Reality and Education

A New Direction for Educational Policy

Daniel Wentland

ROWMAN & LITTLEFIELD EDUCATION
A division of
ROWMAN & LITTLEFIELD PUBLISHERS, INC.
Lanham • New York • Toronto • Plymouth, UK

Published by Rowman & Littlefield Education
A division of Rowman & Littlefield Publishers, Inc.
A wholly owned subsidary of The Rowman & Littlefield Publishing Group, Inc.
4501 Forbes Boulevard, Suite 200, Lanham, Maryland 20706
www.rowman.com

10 Thornbury Road, Plymouth PL6 7PP, United Kingdom

British Library Cataloguing in Publication Information Available

Library of Congress Cataloging-in-Publication Data

Wentland, Daniel.
Reality and education : a new direction for education policy / Daniel Wentland.
pages cm
Includes bibliographical references.
ISBN 978-1-4758-0514-7 (cloth : alk. paper) -- ISBN 978-1-4758-0515-4 (pbk. : alk. paper) -- ISBN 978-1-4758-0516-1 (electronic)
1. Educational planning--United States. 2. Education and state--United States. I. Title.
LC89.W38 2013
371.207--dc23
2013016916

∞™ The paper used in this publication meets the minimum requirements of American
National Standard for Information Sciences Permanence of Paper for Printed Library
Materials, ANSI/NISO Z39.48-1992.

Printed in the United States of America

Contents

Acknowledgments

First, I want to express my appreciation to the readers. I look forward to your comments. Please contact me at danielwentland.com.

Next, a big thanks to Dr. Thomas F. Koerner at Rowman and Littlefield for giving me this opportunity. I hope this will be the beginning of many successful projects we will share together.

Thanks to my editor, Dr. Andrew Kelly, and the editors at Rowman & Littlefield: Carlie Wall, Caitlin Crawford, and Laura Reiter, as well as the rest of the staff at R&L.

On a personal note, thanks to Scarlett and Dakota for the joy they bring my way each day.

Preface

In one of my previous books, I stated that a system is designed to produce the outcomes that are occurring. A poorly designed system produces poor results. Problems with the public education system are reported every day in periodicals and books. Improving student achievement is too important of a societal issue to continue stumbling along the same unending path of "Let's try this educational fad and then move to the next proposed solution."

The uniqueness of this book is that the myths surrounding education and learning are exposed; it's like cleaning the lenses of your glasses so you can get a clear view of the world. Once myths are moved aside, reality can settle in and a practical model for improving education can be developed.

As stated by Milton Friedman, "One of the great mistakes is to judge policies and programs by their intentions rather than their results" (n.d.). The information in this book focuses on outcomes and challenges the paradigms of educators, policymakers, and the public.

A final comment: In Larry Millett's book *Sherlock Holmes and the Red Demon*, Sherlock Holmes is asked the following question: "Now, Mr. Holmes, what will you need to begin your investigation?" Holmes replied, "The facts. They are the foundation of all that will follow" (1996, p. 23). Questions that are not properly answered do not go away. Many educational questions remain a mystery because we fail to face the reality behind those questions. The power of this book is clearly communicating the facts that impact the learning environment and developing models built upon educational realities. *Reality and Education* is a book that will have a dramatic impact upon society, educators, and students.

REFERENCES

Friedman, M. (n.d.). Retrieved September 18, 2012, from http://sphotos-a.xx.fbcdn.net/hpho-tos-prn1/550493_10100414629650916_473350904_n.jpg.
Millett, L. (1996). *Sherlock Holmes and the red demon*. New York: Viking.

Introduction

In the article "Reforming Teaching," the authors assert the following: "On the 1960s TV show 'Gilligan's Island,' one character, the Professor, was always designing ingenious approaches to improve life on the island. Why, the writer Anne Lamott has asked, didn't he just try to fix the boat?" (Darling-Hammond & Haselkorn, 2009, p. 36). Like the Professor, educators suffer from a similar problem. Instead of addressing the core issues that impact the learning environment, too many teachers, administrators, and policymakers have gotten distracted by focusing upon political agendas and superficial educational ideologies. These political and ideological distractions have created a diversion so great that many educators have forgotten what education and learning are truly about. With no direction or purpose, many educators have been reduced to wandering around lost in the desert, chasing after the latest educational fad.

The information in this book brings us out of the desert by moving beyond educational fads, political perspectives, and academic ideologies. Chapters 1 through 10 concentrate on the realities associated with education and learning. Based upon reality, the remaining chapters provide a common-sense analysis for improving educational leadership, school culture, and student achievement.

For those pressed for time, the critical points of each chapter have been summarized at the end of each chapter. These "Critical Points to Remember," like any shortcut, provide an efficient way to capture the information presented in the book. However, although a shortcut is an efficient way to get to your final destination, many of the most interesting and rewarding sights of the journey get missed in your hurry to get from point A to B.

REFERENCE

Darling-Hammond, L., & Haselkorn, D. (2009, April 1). Reforming teaching: Are we missing the boat? *Education Week*, pp. 30, 36.

I

Reality and Education

Chapter One

Focusing on Reality and Education

I love the pursuit of anything and the pursuit of truth is very noble.
—Charles Pellegrino (1988, p. 85)

One of the great mistakes is to judge policies and programs by their intentions rather than their results.
—Milton Friedman (n.d.)

By 1786, five years after George Washington's victory over the British, the American people had lost their way. They were flushed with early success, but desperately unsure of how to hold the Union together.
—Charles Cerami (2005, p. 1)

The uncertainty that clouded the future of the early American republic can be felt today by many Americans who question the quality and cost of public education. For those Americans who once viewed education as the great equalizer that gave individuals an opportunity to succeed, it now seems that educational scholars, practitioners, and policymakers have been reduced to proposing one silver bullet after the next in a never-ending quest to improve student academic performance.

Educators, like puppies racing in circles trying to catch their tails, have fallen into the trap of chasing after the most recent teaching methodology, the "hottest" trends in curriculum theory, or the latest technological innovation. After all that frantic scrambling around, what tends to emerge from those efforts is a series of inconclusive student learning outcomes. Before long, educators turn to the next educational fad, and once again student learning outcomes are mixed. And so the pattern goes, like a long-playing record, with the result always being mediocre student achievement.

This endless cycle of experimentation has not only wasted scarce financial and human resources, but it has also jeopardized the future of many students. The state of preschool, elementary, and secondary education (P–12) has been summarized by Michael Fullan (2005), who states that the "starting point is to observe that nothing tried so far really works" (p. 13).

Problems with public education and the associated financial and non-financial costs to society are reported almost every day in periodicals and books:

- U.S. high school students have not achieved any significant gains in reading or math for nearly four decades (Tomsho, 2009).
- Among workers who have not completed high school, the unemployment rate increased to 15.5%, compared with 8.4% in 2008. By contrast, the jobless rate among those with four-year college degrees was 4.8% (Alini & Lahart, 2009).
- Forty-one percent of students entering community colleges and 29% of all entering college students are not prepared in at least one of the basic skills of reading, writing, and math (Byrd & MacDonald, 2005).
- Students lack the tacit intelligence required to succeed in a college learning environment, including such things as (1) understanding the importance of attending classes, (2) being prepared for class, (3) using course materials, and (4) collaborating with classmates (Smith & Commander, 1997, cited in Byrd & MacDonald, 2005).
- Twenty-two percent of the ACT test takers scored at levels associated with college success in English, math, and science, while only 13% of professors told researchers that their students were very well prepared for college-level work (Olson, 2006).
- High schools do not prepare students for the academic environment and social culture they will be encountering in higher education (Byrd & MacDonald, 2005).
- After nearly 25 years of intensive effort, we have failed to fix our ailing public schools and stem the "rising tide of mediocrity" chronicled in *A Nation at Risk* (Wolk, 2009).
- About 30% of incoming ninth-graders do not graduate from high school in four years. Of the students who go to college, about half of all community college students and one in four students attending a four-year institution leave by the beginning of the second year (Kazis, 2006).
- A reason for the concern about college readiness is the large proportion of high school graduates who end up taking remedial courses in college for which they earn no credit, at considerable cost to themselves and the institution (Olson, 2006).
- Many college faculty members comment that their students are ill prepared for the demands of higher education (Sanoff, 2006).

The following statistics are from McCarthy and Kuh (2006) and Sanoff (2006):

- Of the students who do not complete high school on time, only 27% of the original group of ninth-graders will make it to the second year of college.
- Three-fifths of students in two-year colleges and one quarter in four-year institutions require one or more years of remedial coursework.
- More than one quarter of four-year college students who require three or more remedial classes drop out of college after the first year.
- Only 20 out of any given 100 ninth-graders graduated with an associate's degree within three years or a bachelor's degree within six years.
- In a survey conducted by Maguire Associates, a Boston-area research consulting firm, 84% of the college professors surveyed stated that high school graduates are unprepared or somewhat prepared to pursue a college degree.

The list goes on:

- Only half of the high school students in the nation's 50 largest cities are graduating in four years; about 7 in 10 students are successfully finishing high school in four years; the next generation of workers is not prepared for the global economy; and high school dropouts are disproportionately represented in the criminal justice system, where approximately 75% of state prison inmates did not attain high school diplomas (Fields, 2008).
- The average high school graduation rate is close to 70% (Almeida & Steinberg, 2008).
- In 2007–2008, almost 30,000 schools in the United States failed to make adequate yearly progress, and half of those schools missed achievement goals for two or more years (Hoff, 2009).
- "Many students are not being taught the basics well. Even more are not being challenged intellectually. . . . Because schools are dreary places, too many youngsters drop out" (Lagemann, 2009, p. 44).
- "In the area of turning around troubled schools, we're still lacking the policy and political will to do the job right. We know that at least 5,000 of our schools—about 5% of the total—are seriously underperforming. Among high schools alone, 2,000 are dropout factories. That means that two out of five of their freshmen are not enrolled at the start of their senior year. We know that in thousands of schools serving K–8 children, achievement is low and not improving. If we don't take aggressive action to fix the problems of these schools, we are putting the children in them on track for failure" (Duncan, 2009, p. 36).

Given the dismal statistics, it is time to stop kidding ourselves. As Berger (2009) states, "garbing recycled bad ideas in the new century can't help us, especially when our real problem is that most students haven't mastered the skills that mattered in the last century, and that will continue to matter, like reading and writing" (p. 28).

To develop an educational system that works, we must deal with the realities that lie beneath the learning process. For like the portion of an iceberg that lies below the water, it is what is underneath the waterline that can be extremely dangerous; the ill-fated voyage of the *Titanic* will always serve to remind us of that.

FOCUSING UPON REALITY

In this book the realities associated with education and learning are focused upon, not political crosscurrents or educational ideologies, such as constructivism versus objectivism. These ideologies only serve as distractions from the true purpose of education. As John Kenneth Galbraith (1998) states, "Ideology can be a heavy blanket over thought. Our commitment must always be to thought. Thought must also guide action" (p. 20).

Public schools and educators are among the major disseminators of knowledge and as such have an obligation to encourage a lifelong love affair with learning. Embedded within that obligation is the challenge of coming to grips with reality and what education is and what can be achieved. As a matter of fact, that's the heart of the matter.

CRITICAL POINTS TO REMEMBER

- Questions that are not properly answered do not go away. Many educational questions remain a mystery because we fail to face the reality behind those questions. In other words, we look away from the essential truths that hinder student achievement. As a result, we must ask ourselves if we as a nation truly want to overcome the problems associated with public education (P–12).
- Political crosscurrents and educational ideologies must be peeled away so the reality associated with education and learning can take center stage. Only after we deal with reality can education and learning be maximized. As a matter of fact, that's the heart of the matter.

REFERENCES

Alini, E., & Lahart, J. (2009, June 6–7). The less educated take the worst hit. *Wall Street Journal*, p. A2.

Almeida, C., & Steinberg, A. (2008, July 30). Raising graduation rates in an era of high standards: What states must do. *Education Week*, p. 25.

Berger, P. (2009, April 1). Predicting the past. *Education Week*, pp. 28–29.

Byrd, K. L., & MacDonald, G. (2005, Fall). Defining college readiness from the inside out: First-generation college student perspectives. *Community College Review*, 33(1), pp. 22–37. Retrieved September 20, 2006, from EBSCO host research database.

Cerami, C. (2005). *Young patriots*. Naperville, IL: Sourcebooks.

Duncan, A. (2009, June 17). Start over: Turnarounds should be the first option for low-performing schools. *Education Week*, p. 36.

Fields, G. (2008, October 21). The high school dropout's economic ripple effect. *Wall Street Journal*, p. A13.

Friedman, M. (n.d.). Retrieved September 18, 2012, from http://sphotos-a.xx.fbcdn.net/hphotos-prn1/550493_10100414629650916_473350904_n.jpg.

Fullan, M. (2005). *Leadership and sustainability: System thinkers in action*. Thousand Oaks, CA: Corwin Press.

Galbraith, J. K. (1998). *The socially concerned today*. Toronto: University of Toronto Press.

Hoff, D. (2009, January 7). Schools struggling to meet key goal on accountability: Number failing to make AYP rises 28 percent. *Education Week*, pp. 1, 14–16.

Kazis, R. (2006, Winter). Building a pipeline for college access and success [Electronic version]. *New England Board of Higher Education*, 20(4), pp. 13–15.

Lagemann, E. C. (2009, January 21). Toward a national consensus. *Education Week*, pp. 28, 44.

McCarthy, M., & Kuh, G. D. (2006, May). Are the students ready for college? What student engagement data say [Electronic version]. *Phi Delta Kappan*, 87(9), pp. 664–669.

Olson, L. (2006, April 26). Views differ on defining college preparation. *Education Week*. Retrieved September 20, 2006, from EBSCO host research database.

Pellegrino, C. (1988). *Her Name,* Titanic. New York: Avon Books.

Ravitch, D. (2009, June 10). Time to kill "No Child Left Behind." *Education Week*, pp. 30, 36.

Sanoff, A. P. (2006, March 10). A perception gap over students' preparation. *The Chronicle of Higher Education*, pp. B9–B14. Retrieved September 20, 2006, from EBSCO host research database.

Smith, B. D., and Commander, N. E. (1997). Ideas in practice: Observing academic behaviors for tacit intelligence. *Journal of Developmental Education* 21(1), pp. 31-35.

Tomsho, R. (2009, April 29). Few gains are seen in high school test. *Wall Street Journal*, p. A5.

Wolk, R. (2009, April 22). Why we're still "at risk": The legacy of five faulty assumptions. *Education Week*, pp. 30, 36.

Chapter Two

Not All Students Will Learn at a High Level

All students must understand "the fact that all knowing is uncertain, involves risk, and is grasped and comprehended only through deep, personal commitment of a disciplined search."

—Carl R. Rogers (1983, p. 45)

Professional learning communities (PLCs) and effective school theories are based upon the notion that all students will achieve at a high level of learning. This is a myth, and anyone with common sense can clearly see the lack of truthfulness embedded within the notion. Chasing myths is time consuming and expensive, deflecting resources and priorities away from realistic learning goals and reasonable education policies. As long as education policy is directed toward pie-in-the-sky ideologies, the education community will continue down an unproductive, destructive path, much like an object approaching the event horizon of a black hole. Once caught in an event horizon, nothing can escape, so let's move away from myth chasing and move toward reality.

Reality is reflected in the fact that learning is a complex task. Complex tasks tend to be difficult, nonroutine, or novel. Simple tasks tend to be easy, routine, and standardized. Despite the difficulty associated with a complex task, all students can learn if they so choose. However, the level of learning will be varied. Not all students will earn an A, but all students can increase their knowledge if they put forth the necessary effort.

The two primary reasons that not all students will earn an A are straightforward. The first reason is that not all students are the same. Each student brings a different level of knowledge, skills, abilities, and experiences to the educational setting. Second, there is no guarantee that time and effort will

9

result in accomplishing a complex task. This second reason can be illustrated by Albert Einstein, who, despite his genius, was never able to accomplish the complex task of formulating and quantifying the unified field theory. Thus even the "smartest among us" may lack the human capital to overcome complicated tasks.

DEVELOPING HUMAN CAPITAL

Gary Becker (1964) laid the foundation for the study of human capital acquisition when he distinguished between *general* human capital and *specific* human capital. General human capital has multiple uses and is therefore portable; specific human capital is useful in a narrow line of work and therefore has limited portability. Accordingly, general training is basically an investment in human capital to increase an employee's overall productivity, and it can be transferred to any employment situation. Specific training increases worker productivity only in the job area where the training occurred.

Public education starts the clock in terms of the skills and abilities that future employees will initially bring to the workplace. Thus public education has short-term and long-term cost consequences relating to general and specific human capital development. At the core of human capital development is the learning process. Based upon the work of Bandura (1977), the learning process can be encapsulated within a framework that consists of four components: attention, retention, reproduction, and motivation (see figure 2.1).

IMPROVING LEARNING OUTCOMES SHOULD BE THE ULTIMATE OBJECTIVE OF EDUCATORS

- Attention (gaining awareness; focusing on what is being studied)
- Retention (physical and mental ability to acquire new knowledge, skills, and/or abilities)
- Reproduction (applying new knowledge, skills, and/or abilities)
- Motivation (the desire to learn)

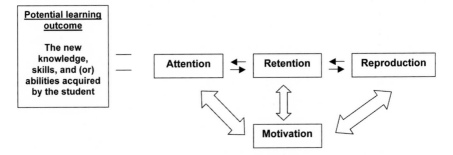

Figure 2.1. Improving Learning Outcomes and Four Components of Learning.

The four components of learning can be rearranged to better illustrate the potential level of learning (see figure 2.2). There is a higher probability that motivated students will learn more and at a faster pace. What the four components of learning demonstrate is that the educational environment should be about learning—period.

IMPLICATIONS FOR A SCHOOL

Some conclusions or recommendations regarding student learning in a school setting are these:

- Reinforce proper actions, behaviors, and statements. Improper actions, behaviors, and statements should be discouraged.
- Students learn best when they understand the objective of the educational program. The educational objective should consist of three components: (1) an explanation of what the student is expected to do (performance); (2) a statement of the quality or level of performance that is acceptable (criterion); and (3) a declaration of the conditions under which the student is expected to perform the desired outcome (conditions). In sum, specific objectives or goals that should be achieved must be identified.
- Students tend to learn better when the educational experience is linked to their current life situation because this enhances the meaningfulness of the learning situation.
- Students are more motivated to learn when they have input into the characteristics of the learning situation, such as goal setting and project selection.
- Students learn best when they have the opportunity to practice. The teacher should identify and explain three things: (1) what the students will be doing when practicing the objectives (performance); (2) the criteria for attainment of the objective; and (3) the conditions under which the practice session(s) will be conducted. The educational experience might be

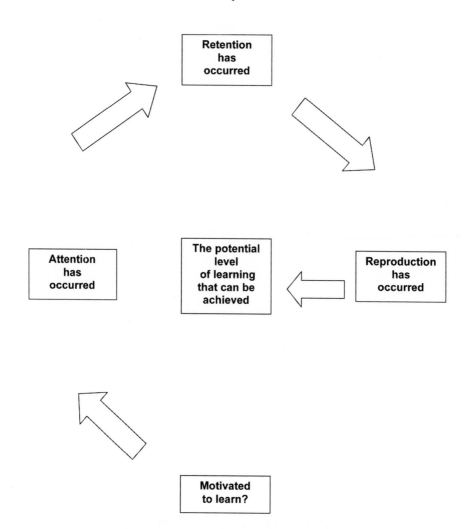

Figure 2.2.   Rearrangement of the Four Components of Learning.

further enhanced by teachers providing students with opportunities to choose their practice strategy.
- Students need feedback. To be effective, the feedback should be specific and be provided as soon as possible.
- Students learn by observing and imitating a technique or model. For a technique or model to be effective, the desired solution, behaviors, or skills need to be clearly specified. After observing the technique or model, students should have the opportunity to reproduce the technique or imitate the skills and behaviors illustrated by the model.

- Students need the curriculum and classroom to be properly coordinated and arranged. Good coordination ensures that students are not distracted by an uncomfortable room, poorly organized materials, or anything else that might interfere with learning.
- Learning is most likely to occur when a student believes that his or her effort will lead to a particular outcome. The outcome should be valued by the student.
- Student learning can be enhanced if the teacher keeps the attention of the students focused on what is being modeled or studied. The teacher should understand how incentives and motivational processes can positively or negatively influence retention and reproduction.

To conclude, learning is the formal or informal process of acquiring new knowledge, skills, or abilities. According to Snowman and Biehler (2006), "knowledge is remembering previous learned information, such as facts, terms, procedures, and principles" (p. 349). The accumulation of knowledge, skills, and abilities requires time, persistence, and effort. This is the first reality regarding education and learning. Those students who do not acknowledge this truth will lack a realistic view of what it takes to succeed academically. Educators who do not inform their students of the first reality regarding education and learning are doing a great disservice to their students.

CRITICAL POINTS TO REMEMBER

- Learning is a complex task that requires time, persistence, and effort. Not everyone will accomplish a complex task. This is the first reality regarding education and learning. Thus not all students will earn an A.
- The four components of learning are:

  1. attention;
  2. retention;
  3. reproduction; and
  4. motivation.

- Student learning implications include:

  1. reinforcing proper actions, behaviors, and statements in the classroom;
  2. allowing students to learn by watching others who act as models;
  3. keeping the attention of a student focused on what is being modeled or studied in a curriculum unit;

4. understanding how incentives and motivational processes can positively or negatively influence student learning;
5. identifying specific academic objectives and goals that must be mastered;
6. addressing individual student learning needs or deficiencies;
7. understanding that learning is most likely to occur when a student believes that his or her effort will lead to a particular outcome and when the outcome is valued by the student;
8. linking educational learning objectives to the student's current life situation;
9. allowing students to practice in order to improve learning outcomes;
10. providing academic feedback and specific behavior corrections as soon as possible;
11. preparing well-designed curriculum and course content prior to presenting the information in the classroom;
12. arranging the classroom (seating, equipment, and so forth) to facilitate the learning process; and
13. ensuring that grading and course content are fair and objective.

REFERENCES

Bandura, A. (1977). *Social learning theory*. Upper Saddle River, NJ: Prentice-Hall.

Becker, G. (1964). *Human capital*. New York: Columbia University Press.

Rogers, C. (2008). Freedom to learn for the eighties. In *Taking sides: Clashing views on educational issues*, 14th ed., J. W. Noll (Ed.). Dubuque, IA: McGraw-Hill, pp. 40-47.

Snowman, J., & Biehler, R. (2006). *Psychology applied to teaching*. 11th ed. Boston: Houghton Mifflin.

Chapter Three

The Role of Education

I challenge you open your mind. . . . See the proof that has always been there, in front of you, only you didn't know how to recognize it for what it was.
—R. J. Pineiro (1999, p. 123)

We've tried just about everything: smaller schools, year-round schools, single-sex classes, after-school mentoring, school uniforms, charter and magnet schools, school–business partnerships, merit pay for teachers, payments to students for performance, private management companies and for-profit schools, takeovers by mayors and state departments of education, site-based management, data-based decision making, and just about every idea containing the words "standards" and "accountability." All of these suggested silver bullets promised results, but little has changed.
—Joseph Renzulli (2008, p. 30)

School reform hasn't made a sustainable difference in student achievement because educators, policymakers, and the community at large have failed to confront what really matters in education. As a consequence, a series of bandages have been put on public education (i.e., new fads), but the underlying realities of education are never acknowledged. Bandages don't heal an illness. It is diagnosing and addressing the root cause of the problem that cures the patient.

In education there are many unresolved issues because we as a nation have failed to address the root causes that impact the effectiveness of education and learning. As previously stated, *questions that are not properly answered will not go away*. Educational questions remain a mystery because we fail to face the reality behind those questions. In other words, we look away from the essential truths that hinder student achievement. It is easier to hide from the realities associated with learning, education, and student achievement than to confront the facts openly and honestly. It might not be political-

15

ly correct to tell it like it is, however, to move from the shadows and into the light of sustainable student achievement, we can no longer afford to look away from the mirror of educational truth.

In the second chapter, the first reality regarding learning and education began the process of moving toward the light by highlighting a fact associated with student achievement. No sugar coating; just the truth. Learning is a complex task that requires time, persistence, and effort. For those students who refuse to work extremely hard, the probability of academic success is unlikely.

Realizing that many educators and policymakers may not want to accept the facts regarding education goes a long way toward explaining the underrealization of human potential that is so often a product of public education. When one doesn't face reality, then problems are bound to follow.

THE UNDERREALIZATION VERSUS THE REALIZATION OF HUMAN POTENTIAL

There can be no greater task than to extinguish the underrealization of human potential. Why aren't schools places where the human potential of all students can be realized? Why has education been turned upside down, or inside out if you prefer, by the fostering of the underrealization of human potential instead of the realization of human potential? This upside-down situation is one of the major criticisms haunting public education; "given the complexity of the institution of education, and the fads, ideologies, theories, economic agendas, political crosscurrents, and unexamined assumptions" (Brady, 2008, pp. 27 & 29), it's no wonder that educational results have been mixed.

Navigating the world of education is like sailing on a rudderless boat and being blown by the wind in one direction and then another. You might travel a long distance but will likely never arrive at your intended destination. The loss of direction in education can be traced to the confusion over what it is supposed to be, how it is best achieved, and the obstacles that must be overcome.

Several educational ideologies have emerged: perennialism, essentialism, progressivism, critical theory, multicultural education, constructivism, and objectivism. Each provides an alternative approach for understanding the role of education. For example, according to the educational theory of perennialism, important truths do not change over time. Educational programs should focus upon unchanging principles, and vocational training should not be emphasized.

Essentialism suggests there is a core of essential knowledge, primarily derived from scientific and technical fields, that must be mastered by all students. Essentially, the most valued knowledge is that which is practical and useful.

Progressivism is a philosophy that views change as the essence of reality and promotes the view that schools should develop learners' problem-solving skills to help students cope with change.

Critical theory is a contemporary extension of social reconstructionism. This theory of education advocates utilizing schools to engineer a new society and transform existing social inequalities and injustices.

Multicultural education seeks educational equity for all students by requiring a curriculum that accurately illustrates how various cultures have influenced Western civilization. All students should develop a multicultural perspective.

Constructivism suggests that students control their learning. A major belief of constructivism is that knowledge is subjective and relative to the individual or community. "Constructivism is an approach to learning in which students construct new understandings through active engagement with their past and present experiences" (Noll, 2008, pp. 50–51).

Objectivism asserts that knowledge has an independent existence according to an objectivist view (Carson, 2005). Objectivism is an educational ideology that emphasizes knowledge absorption by passive learners (Noll, 2008, p. 51).

The following summarizes other interpretations of what education is supposed to be:

• "In the early history of our public education developing good character . . . was considered essential. . . . But in the last part of the 20th century, most public schools drifted away from that tradition. . . . Fortunately, in the past two decades, the character education movement has revived" (McDonnell, 2008, p. 25).
• The key to "success may lie in their commitment to a broad curriculum, with healthy doses of liberal arts and sciences," while "many American schools are, in contrast, sacrificing the arts and humanities because of pressure to improve reading and mathematics scores" (Cavanagh, 2009, p. 12).
• In some countries "content is king," while critics argue that the focus should be on "more meaningful objectives, such as learning how to think critically" (Manzo, 2008, p. 23).
• "Today, many argue, or simply assume, that the primary purpose of public education is economic: to get a better job. The economic purpose is to prepare workers to compete in our free-market system." Others suggest that the "primary purpose of public education is to prepare students to participate effectively as citizens in our constitutional democracy" (McClung, 2008, pp. 30–31).

Some educators believe the following five assumptions should be the bedrock of education. Other researchers proclaim that the assumptions are fallacies (Wolk, 2009, pp. 30 & 36):

- Rigorous content standards should be established, preferably on a national basis.
- Standardized test scores are accurate measures of student achievement and should be the basis for determining promotion and graduation.
- Highly qualified teachers should be in every classroom.
- All students should be required to take algebra in the eighth grade and higher-order math in high school in order to increase the number of scientists and engineers.
- Reducing the student dropout rate can be achieved by ending social promotion, funding dropout prevention programs, and increasing the mandatory attendance age.

- "In the United States, education typically refers to formal education in school settings. It is associated with doing well academically and demonstrating that ability through good grades" (Rothstein-Fisch & Trumbull, 2008, p. 13). Other definitions assert that education should "produce a good and knowledgeable person, one who respects other people and does not place self above others in importance" (Valdes, 1996, cited by Rothstein-Fisch & Trumbull, 2008, p. 13). Competency-based education (CBE) "reflects the ability to do something as compared to the traditional ability to demonstrate knowledge" (Finch & Crunkilton, 1989, p. 242). Another definition is that public education is a "social system established to deliver good education to the students who attend it" (Kretovics & Nussel, 1994, p. 99).
- The problems with education include: (1) lack of funding, (2) dropout rates, (3) the achievement gap for minority students, (4) shortage of qualified teachers, (5) lack of discipline, and (6) drugs (Brimley & Garfield, 2008, pp. 35, 38).
- The purpose of education is to promote social-emotional-mental growth (improve man as man) versus traditional intellectual training, meaning the chief business of the school is to transmit knowledge and skills to the next generation (Dewey, 1938, and Hutchins, 1953, pp. 4 & 11).
- Various approaches to teaching include: (1) devising and using instructional objectives that specify observable, measurable student behaviors; (2) a behavioral approach (direct instruction) focusing upon learning basic skills, with the teacher making all decisions, keeping students on task, and emphasizing positive reinforcement; (3) a cognitive approach facilitating meaningful learning in which students discover how to be autonomous, self-directed learners; (4) a humanistic approach that "pays particular attention to the role of noncognitive variables in learning, specifically, stu-

dent needs, emotions, values, and self-perceptions" (Snowman & Biehler, 2006, p. 370); and (5) a social approach stressing how students can learn from each other.
- The values of equity, efficiency, choice, and excellence have at various times been overemphasized at the expense of the others (Sergiovanni, Kelleher, McCarthy, & Wirt, 2004).

So what can be gleaned from this array of confusing ideologies, definitions, philosophies, stated purposes, theories, assumptions, viewpoints, and problems with education? It seems that somewhere among the cluster, the basic role of education has been lost. This loss of identity is the second reality associated with education and learning. However, like the phoenix rising from the ashes, it is the confusion and loss of direction that provides us with an opportunity to change education. Paul Davies (1988) states, "The fact that the universe is full of complexity does not mean that the underlying laws are also complex" (p. 63). The same reasoning can be applied to education.

Given the second reality of education and learning, it is clear that educational scholars, practitioners, and policymakers must agree on the definition of education and its role in society. To begin clarifying the role of education, the following statements are offered:

- Formal education is a structured system (process and environment) in which learning occurs. As defined in chapter 2, learning is acquiring new knowledge, skills, or abilities.
- The purpose of formal education is to maximize the learning environment—period.
- To accomplish the purpose of formal education, the realities associated with learning and education must be acknowledged, and educational decisions must be driven by those realities, not ideology.

More specifics are provided in later chapters. For now, let's conclude with a statement from Virginia Miller (2001):

> America is embroiled in a debate over how best to educate its students. Throughout the past three decades, elementary and secondary students have been exposed to a sea of educational fads, from new math and whole language to outcome-based education and cooperative learning. Each new theory has been administered as a healing elixir for the failure of public schools to help American youth rise to the same heights as many foreign students on international achievement measures. (p. 24)

Miller's message is unfortunately as accurate today as it was in 2001. The definition and purpose of education, the function of curriculum, and the roles of students and teachers have gotten lost among all the educational ideologies and political crosscurrents that have evolved. This is the second reality associated with education and learning: Education has lost its identity. If educational scholars, practitioners, and policymakers do not acknowledge the truths about education and learning, then the underrealization of human potential will continue to be the end product of the educational process.

CRITICAL POINTS TO REMEMBER

- Navigating the world of education is like sailing on a rudderless boat and being blown by the wind in one direction then another. The loss of direction in education can be traced to all the confusion over the various educational ideologies and political crosscurrents that have evolved. This confusion is the second reality associated with learning and education. Education's lost identity has resulted in the underrealization of human potential.
- Given the second reality associated with education and learning, it is clear that educational scholars, practitioners, and policymakers must agree on what education is and what its role in society should be.

To start the process of clearing away the clutter regarding the definition and purpose of education, the following statements are offered:

- Formal education is a structured system (process and environment) in which learning occurs. As defined in chapter 2, learning is acquiring new knowledge, skills, or abilities.
- The purpose of formal education is to maximize the learning environment—period.
- To accomplish the purpose of formal education, the realities associated with learning and education must be acknowledged, and those realities must drive policymaking.

REFERENCES

Brady, M. (2008, February 27). A "21st-century education": What does it mean? *Education Week*, pp. 27, 29.
Brimley, V., & Garfield, R. (2008). *Financing education in a climate of change*. 10th ed., Boston: Allyn & Bacon/Pearson Education.
Carson, J. (2005, Spring). Objectivism and education: A response to David Elkind's "The problem with constructivism." *The Educational Forum*, 69, pp. 232–238.
Cavanagh, S. (2009, June 10). Nations performing at top committed to broad curriculum. *Education Week*, p. 12.
Davies, P. (1988). *The cosmic blueprint: New discoveries in nature's creative ability to order the universe*. New York: Touchstone Books.
Dewey, J. (2008). Experience and education. In *Taking sides: Clashing views on educational issues*. 14th ed., J. W. Noll (Ed.). Dubuque, IA: McGraw-Hill, pp. 4–10.

Finch, C., & Crunkilton, J. (1989). *Curriculum development in vocational and technical education: Planning, content, and implementation.* 3rd ed. Needham Heights, MS: Allyn and Bacon.

Hutchins, R. (2008). The conflict in education in a democratic society. In *Taking sides: Clashing views on educational issues.* 14th ed., J. W. Noll (Ed.). Dubuque, IA: McGraw-Hill, pp. 11-14.

Kretovics, J., & Nussel, E. (1994). *Transforming urban education.* Boston: Allyn & Bacon.

Manzo, K. (2008, May 21). Learning essentials. *Education Week*, pp. 23–25.

McClung, M. (2008, December 3). The civil standard: An alternative to No Child Left Behind. *Education Week*, pp. 30–31.

McDonnell, S. (2008, October 8). America's crisis of character—and what to do about it. *Education Week*, p. 25.

Miller, V. (2001, July). School-to-work education shortchange academic knowledge. *USA Today Magazine*, 130(2674): 24–27. Retrieved April 3, 2008, from EBSCO host research database.

Noll, J. W. (2008). In *Taking sides: Clashing views on educational issues.* 14th ed., J. W. Noll (Ed.). Dubuque, IA: McGraw-Hill.

Pineiro, R. J. (1999). *01-01-00: A novel of the millennium.* New York: Forge.

Renzulli, J. (2008, July 16). Engagement is the answer. *Education Week*, pp. 30–31.

Rothstein-Fisch, C., & Trumbull, E. (2008). *Managing diverse classrooms: How to build on students' cultural strengths.* Alexandria, VA: ASCD.

Sergiovanni, T., Kelleher, P., McCarthy, M., & Wirt, F. (2004). *Educational governance and administration.* 5th ed. Boston: Pearson/Allyn & Bacon.

Snowman, J., & Biehler, R. (2006). *Psychology applied to teaching.* 11th ed. Boston: Houghton Mifflin.

Valdes, G. (1996). *Con respeto: Bridging the distances between culturally diverse families and schools: An ethnographic portrait.* New York: Teachers College Press.

Wolk, R. (2009, April 22). Why we're still at risk: The legacy of five faulty assumptions. *Education Week*, pp. 30, 36.

Chapter Four

Look for Teachers Who Love to Learn

Outcome is often determined by the manner in which something is presented.
—Steve Alton (1999, p. 40)

I guess my point is that there's never been a time when I didn't live for information, and I've always felt that, for me at least, learning and growing is the primary purpose of life.
—Thorne (2004, p. 302)

To the teachers reading this book, I ask the following questions:

- Do your actions reflect the sentiments voiced in the statement by Thorne?
- Do you love to learn?
- Are you committed to improving yourself?

If you answered no to any of those, how can you convince your students to love to learn or develop a desire for self-improvement?

TEACHING AND STUDENT ACHIEVEMENT

Quality teaching and student achievement appear to be closely correlated:

- "The classroom teacher is crucial to learning" (Cuban, 2009, p. 30).
- "Well-prepared and well-supported teachers are important for all students but especially for students who come to school with greater needs" (Darling-Hammond & Berry, 2006, p. 15).
- "The skills and knowledge of teachers and support professionals are the greatest determinant of how well students learn" (Weaver, 2006, p. 34).

- "Despite all the evidence that teachers matter most in student achieve-ment, the most damaging practice in all of U.S. education persists: giving poor and minority students the least access to high-quality teaching" (Hay-cock, 2006, p. 41).
- Student achievement "has everything to do with the quality of instruction in the classroom" (Rhee, 2007, cited in Maxwell, 2007, p. 18).
- "An effective teacher can contribute substantially to student achievement, regardless of students' innate abilities and home and neighborhood socio-economic circumstances" (Guthrie & Schuermann, 2008, p. 24).
- "Research by scholars such as Ronald F. Ferguson, Linda Darling-Ham-mond, Richard M. Ingersoll, William L. Sanders, Kati Haycock, and oth-ers shows that teacher quality is the most important variable in student achievement that schools can affect" (Beatty, 2008, p. 40).
- "The research evidence that teachers matter is overwhelming" (Haycock, 2008, cited in Sawchuk, 2008, p. 6).
- "Over the past two decades, researchers of all ideological stripes and methodological perspectives have converged around a view that teachers are the key to whether or not students achieve" (Berry, 2009, p. 28).
- "Almost everyone recognizes the importance of effective teachers" (Ol-son, 2007, p. 9).
- "Researchers agree that good teachers are the single most important factor in kids' school success" (Mishel, Allegretto, & Corcoran, 2008, p. 30).

The vital connection between good teaching and student academic perfor-mance is best illustrated by an anonymous e-mail that I received. The email was titled "What Teachers Make":

> The dinner guests were sitting around the table discussing life. One man, a CEO, decided to explain the problem with education. He argued, "What's a kid going to learn from someone who decided his best option in life was to become a teacher?" He reminded the other dinner guests what they say about teachers: "Those who can't do something teach." To stress his point he said to another guest; "You're a teacher, Bonnie. Be honest. What do you make?"
>
> Bonnie, who had a reputation for honesty and frankness, replied, "You want to know what I make?" She paused for a second, then began: "Well, I make kids work harder than they ever thought they could. I make a C+ feel like the Congressional Medal of Honor. I make kids sit through 40 minutes of class time when their parents can't make them sit for 5 without an iPod, Game Cube or movie rental. You want to know what I make?" She paused again and looked at each and every person at the table:
>
> - I make kids wonder.
> - I make them question.
> - I make them criticize.
> - I make them apologize and mean it.

- I make them have respect and take responsibility for their actions.
- I teach them to write and then I make them write.
- I make them read, read, read.
- I make them show all their work in math.
- I make my students from other countries learn everything they need to know in English while preserving their unique cultural identity.
- I make my classroom a place where all my students feel safe.
- I make my students stand to say the Pledge of Allegiance to the flag because we live in the United States of America.
- Finally, I make them understand that if they use the gifts they were given, work hard, and follow their hearts, they can succeed in life.

Bonnie paused one last time and then continued, "Then, when people try to judge me by what I make, I can hold my head up high and pay no attention because they are ignorant. You want to know what I make? *I make a difference. What do you make?*"

Unfortunately, in the real world of education, there might be many teachers who do not make a difference. Recently, Cech (2008) reported that 40% of teachers felt that outstanding teachers should not be "especially rewarded" for their stellar performance. Additionally, only 48% of the teachers stated that outstanding teachers should be "especially rewarded." Just 48%; that's shocking.

Rewarding top-performing individuals can be a serious problem if group norms enforce mediocre performance. Norms are acceptable standards of behavior within a group that are shared by the group's members. Unproductive group norms promote mediocre performance, and mediocrity is unacceptable in teaching. Teachers who don't have a thirst for learning jeopardize the level of learning that will occur within a classroom. Uninspiring teachers decrease the chance of sparking a longing for learning in their students. Encouraging students to want to learn and expand their knowledge, skills, and abilities brings us to the third reality associated with education and learning: A highly qualified teacher is a lifelong learner who knows subject content and can inspire students to learn.

TEACHERS WHO MAKE A DIFFERENCE

All teachers should consider the following questions:

- When was the last time you longed to learn about anything new and then actively pursued that longing?
- What coursework have you taken recently that was not mandated?
- Do you regularly keep up to date on general educational issues, subject matter, and curriculum development?

• Do you make a difference in the classroom? In other words, how does your teaching impact students? How are students who leave your classroom different from the individuals who entered your classroom?

The answers to these and similar questions determine whether you have a passion for learning that can awe and motivate others to want to learn. A highly qualified teacher generates a "learning frenzy" in the classroom, which stimulates a frantic drive in each student to want to know more and become a better person.

CRITICAL POINTS TO REMEMBER

• For one to inspire, one needs to be inspired.
• The third reality regarding education and learning is that a highly qualified teacher is a lifelong learner who knows subject content and can inspire students to learn. A teacher who loves to learn has a higher probability of igniting that same passion for learning in his or her students.

REFERENCES

Alton, S. (1999). *The trench.* New York: Kensington.
Beatty, B. (2008, November 12). How the bad economy could produce better teachers. *Education Week*, p. 40.
Berry, B. (2009, May 20). Ending the battles over teaching: Ways we can work together to enhance the profession's future. *Education Week*, pp. 24, 28.
Cech, S. (2008, May 14). Poll finds U.S. teachers split on role of unions, pay incentives, tenure. *Education Week*, p. 9.
Cuban, L. (2009, April 29). Hugging the middle: Why good teaching ignores ideology. *Education Week*, pp. 30–31.
Darling-Hammond, L., & Berry, B. (2006, November). Highly qualified teachers for all. *Educational Leadership* 64(3), p. 15.
Guthrie, J., & Schuermann, P. (2008, October 29). The question of performance pay: What we know, what we don't know, and what we need to know. *Education Week*, pp. 24–26.
Haycock, K. (2006, November). No more invisible kids. *Educational Leadership* 64(3), pp. 38–42.
Maxwell, L. (2007, June 20). Mayor takes control, picks novice to lead troubled D.C. district. *Education Week*, p. 18.
Mishel, L., Allegretto, S., & Corcoran, S. (2008, April 30). The teaching penalty: We can't recruit and retain excellent educators on the cheap. *Education Week*, p. 30.
Olson, L. (2007, April 11). Scholars suggest policies to bolster teacher quality: Approaches range from pay incentives to better training and conditions. *Education Week*, p. 9.
Sawchuk, S. (2008, December 10). Out-of-field teaching more common in poor schools. *Education Week*, p. 6.
Thorne, T. (2004). *Thunder road.* New York: Kensington/Pinnacle Books.
Weaver, R. (2006, November). A positive agenda for ESEA. *Educational Leadership* 64(3), p. 34.

Chapter Five

Students Have a Role to Play

Students bring their own attitudes and motivations to the classroom, and as a consequence, their decisions about education and learning have an important impact about what will occur in the classroom.

—Daniel Wentland

When we read about the lack of student academic performance, the blame is usually attributed to poor teaching. If only the teachers were better, the students would have passed. Less frequently mentioned are (1) the school culture and structure under which teachers must perform their jobs, (2) the lack of support from the parents and community, and (3) the confusing assortment of educational ideologies and political crosscurrents. Rarely or never mentioned is the lack of persistence and effort on the part of the student. The student is portrayed as the victim of an uninspired teacher, doomed from the start.

This "blame anything other than ourselves" mentality is reflected in our current society. Few people take personal responsibility for anything—it is always the other person or whatever we wish to blame that caused our failure or problem. If only he or she or it would go away, then everything would be okay. In short, few individuals hold themselves accountable for their actions.

In terms of education, let's wake up and understand that students have an equal responsibility in their learning. Every student makes the decision whether to learn or not. Those students who decide that education and learning are important will succeed despite any barrier put in their way. It is a personal choice to want to succeed. Whether we want to accept this fact or not, decisions are a part of life, and individuals must accept the responsibility for their decisions. Let's stop passing the buck; the buck stops with each of us.

In his best-selling book *The Seven Habits of Highly Effective People* (1989), Stephen Covey writes about an individual in a Nazi concentration camp. Despite all the horrors the man witnessed and suffered, he made the decision not to let his captors rob him of his spirit. In the end he succeeded. The same is true for all students. Despite any condition (internal or external to the school), each student holds the key to the eventual outcome. In life, as well as in education, if you want something badly enough, are willing to work hard, and are persistent, good things generally happen. It may not be the exact outcome that was envisioned, but success tends to come your way.

As an educator, part of your job is to help students understand that they have a critical decision to make; do they want to succeed academically or not? Their decision will be a major determinant of what will happen in the classroom.

IN THE END, IT'S THE STUDENT'S RESPONSIBILITY TO LEARN

The fourth reality associated with education and learning is that students play an important role in their own learning by making the decision to want to learn. Those students who make the decision that learning is important will increase the probability of greater academic success than those who decide not to put forth the time, effort, and persistence that is necessary to learn. When it's all said and done, it's the student's responsibility to learn.

A few years ago, I was taking a class, and the teacher was talking about the various types of students he had encountered over his years of teaching. The teacher suggested six types of students:

1. Rather be somewhere else
2. Does as little as possible (does the minimum)
3. Finds as much fault as possible except for themselves
4. Substitutes excuses for actions (never gets the work done or is always late with assignments)
5. Lacks the knowledge, skills, abilities, and educational preparedness to successfully understand and learn the material
6. Gets the job done (a mature student who puts the time and effort in)

The six types of students outlined by this teacher is reality, and let's face it: Spending enormous amounts of money and other resources on students who do not want to learn has been a disaster. Schools and teachers must do what can be done to encourage learning, but in the end, it is the decision of the student.

CRITICAL POINTS TO REMEMBER

- The fourth reality regarding education and learning is that the student is responsible for his or her learning.
- Students' decisions about how much time and effort they are willing to put forth are as important as any other factor impacting learning. Students (just like schools, administrators, and teachers) must be held accountable for their decisions.

REFERENCE

Covey, S. (1989). *The seven habits of highly effective people.* New York: Fireside.

Chapter Six

Look for an Administrator Who Is the Right Type of Leader

"A leader inspires individuals and groups to do their best. A successful manager pursues organizational goals and objectives in such a way that the growth and integrity of people are respected" (Johnston, 1994, cited in Seyfarth, 1999, p. 11). A school administrator needs to be a leader and a successful manager if student learning is going to be maximized.

—Daniel Wentland

In 1996, the Council of Chief State Officers suggested six standards for school administrators:

1. A school administrator is an educational leader who promotes the success of all students by facilitating the development, articulation, implementation, and stewardship of a vision of learning that is shared and supported by the school community.
2. A school administrator is an educational leader who promotes the success of all students by advocating, nurturing, and sustaining a school culture and instructional program conducive to student learning and staff professional growth.
3. A school administrator is an educational leader who promotes the success of all students by ensuring management of the organization, operations, and resources for a safe, efficient, and effective learning environment.
4. A school administrator is an educational leader who promotes the success of all students by collaborating with families and community members, responding to diverse community interests and needs, and mobilizing community resources.

5. A school administrator is an educational leader who promotes the success of all students by acting with integrity, fairness, and in an ethical manner.
6. A school administrator is an educational leader who promotes the success of all students by understanding, responding to, and influencing the larger political, social, economic, legal, and cultural context.

Despite the publication of these standards, the educational environment is characterized by numerous underperforming P–12 schools, while at many colleges and universities a relationship of distrust and animosity exists between administrators and faculty. Given this dismal picture, it is impossible to ignore the impact of educational leadership upon the learning process.

Unfortunately, many school administrators have limited exposure to managerial principles and lack the training to lead and motivate others. Organizations guided by poor managers produce at best mediocre products. When examining marginally performing organizations, a vital aspect of the analysis focuses upon the managerial philosophy, structure, and practices that control how the organization operates. Developing effective educational administrators at the P–12 level who understand managerial and leadership fundamentals is a vital piece of the educational puzzle.

MANAGEMENT AND LEADERSHIP

At the end of the movie *High Plains Drifter*, the leader of a notorious gang of outlaws is frantically looking from side to side in the hope of spotting a fast-shooting, mysterious drifter. With sweat dripping off his chin and fear filling his eyes, the villain shouts in a desperate tone, "Who are you?" The only response from the drifter is a bullet that ends the villain's life. Hell is the next stop for the outlaw.

Fortunately for us, we do not have to engage in a violent struggle between the forces of good and evil, but life does force us to wrestle with the concepts of perception, personality, attitudes, and motivation as well as various economic factors. It is the mixing together of these concepts that molds us into who we are, just like a sculptor chisels upon a piece of marble until the desired form is achieved. The end result for the sculptor is a work of art. The final outcome for an individual is the development of a particular approach to life. Every human being tends to view life from one of two perspectives: egocentric or altruistic. These two perspectives or approaches to life not only define who we are but can also function as a framework for understanding what it takes to be the right type of leader.

UNDERSTANDING WHO WE ARE AND IN THE PROCESS DISCOVERING THE RIGHT TYPE OF LEADER

Let us consider two individuals. The first person is (1) highly materialistic; (2) always focused upon his or her needs; (3) only concerned with achieving goals, not with how the goals are accomplished; (4) never thinking about the future; (5) insensitive toward the physical environment (meaning at the macro level the Earth and its resources as well as at the micro level the workplace); (6) not interested in anyone else's point of view; (7) power driven; and finally (8) constantly favoring certain individuals. The second person has the opposite characteristics.

Which individual would you prefer as a boss? I don't believe anyone would select the first individual, and if you were unfortunate enough to have to work for that type of person, how much effort would you put forth? The first individual has the characteristics associated with an egocentric view of life. The second person has adopted an altruistic view of life. The right type of leader must possess an altruistic perspective of life, for only that kind of person will have the characteristics that are necessary to inspire others to want to do their best.

An egocentric person is primarily consumed with satisfying his or her own needs. An altruistic person focuses upon the interests of others and as a result gains the trust and loyalty of those who work for them. It is that bond of trust and loyalty between the altruistic leader and the employees that sets the foundation for obtaining extraordinary organizational results. Put simply, in terms of achieving organizational success and sustainability, an individual with an egocentric approach to life will in the long run never measure up to a person with an altruistic viewpoint.

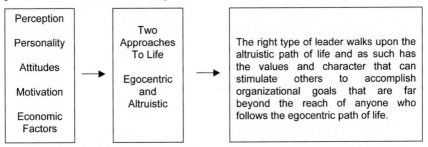

Figure 6.1.   Understanding Who We Are and in the Process Discovering the Right Kind of Leadership.

Given the importance of leadership in terms of organizational success and sustainability, what exactly is leadership? Unfortunately a straightforward definition has proven elusive, for *leadership* has been defined in many ways by many individuals:

- "Leadership is both a process and a property. As a process, leadership involves the use of noncoercive influences. As a property, leadership is the set of characteristics attributed to someone who is perceived to use influence successfully" (Moorhead & Griffin, 1995, p. 297).
- "Leadership is the process whereby one person influences others to work toward a goal and helps them pursue a vision" (Yulk & VanFleet, 1992, cited in Hellriegel, Slocum, & Woodman, 1995, p. 342).
- Leadership is the process of guiding and motivating others toward the achievement of organizational goals (Gitman & McDaniel, 2003, p. 173).
- "Strategic leadership refers to the ability to articulate a strategic vision for the company, or a part of the company, and to motivate others to buy into that vision" (Hill & Jones, 1998, p. 14).
- "Leadership is the ability to influence a group toward the achievement of goals" (Robbins, 2001, p. 314).
- "Leadership . . . is the ability to get other people to get the very best out of themselves. And it is manifested . . . not by getting them to follow you, but by getting them to join you. You don't get the best out of people by bulldozing them; you do it by educating (or convincing) them" (Levy, 2004, p. 339).
- "Leadership requires distinct behaviors and attitudes. . . . When you become a leader, success is all about growing others" (Welch & Welch, 2005, p. 45).

And the list can go on and on, but in the end, the definition isn't important. What matters is that the right type of leader is in place, meaning an individual who pursues organizational goals and objectives in such a way that the growth and integrity of people are respected (Johnston, 1994, cited in Seyfarth, 1999). The specific characteristics of the right type of leader include:

- The right type of leader has the right self-image and self-concept to want to create a workplace in which the traditional management–employee relationship paradigm is cast aside in favor of the new management–employee paradigm, meaning that employees are regarded as partners, not subordinates. In other words, management must put employees first and mean it. Management retains the final decision-making authority, but the focus should be upon how an organizational decision impacts the employees, for that in turn will influence how the employees perform their job and ultimately how they interact with the customer.
- The right type of leader can easily adapt to various situations and is sociable, conscientious, tactful, considerate, and open to various points of view.
- The right type of leader is not interested in himself (or herself) but instead is focused upon the conditions of all those individuals who work for them.

By truly caring about the employees, the right type of leader will achieve unparalleled organizational success. In other words, the right type of leader makes a true commitment to the employees, and it is that commitment that inspires the employees to want to accomplish organizational goals in the most effective and efficient manner (social exchange theory).

- The right type of leader embraces change, whether it is small or large, whenever it is necessary to do so. In fact, the right type of leader actively promotes an organizational culture that has an enhanced capacity to learn, adapt, and change.
- The right type of leader possesses an altruistic perspective on life, for only that kind of person has the characteristics to inspire others to want to do their best.
- The right type of leader pursues organizational goals and objectives in such a way that the growth and integrity of people are respected.

Now let us summarize the characteristics of a leader with a leadership style that flows from an egocentric perspective of life. This can best be described as a CREEPS approach to leadership:

- CREEPS are *control freaks*. CREEPS make all the decisions and make only a token or superficial effort to seek employee input or suggestions. CREEPS are the ultimate micromanagers. Anything not initiated by CREEPS is rejected.
- CREEPS form *relationships* with favorite employees; work performance is secondary. Only those in the inner circle of CREEPS are allowed any involvement in the day-to-day managerial activities of the organization.
- CREEPS have king- or queen-size *egos* and view employees as cogs in a machine that can be easily replaced. CREEPS have very little or no concern for employees except for the CREEPS' favorite employees. CREEPS utilize human resource policies to intimidate and severely limit employee empowerment.
- CREEPS have limited *ethics*. CREEPS utilize a Machiavellian approach to getting tasks accomplished. CREEPS are abusive and manipulative. CREEPS are concerned only about themselves and view others as human pawns that can be used as CREEPS see fit; any employee development will only occur if it benefits the CREEPS.
- CREEPS love *power* and institute a top-down managerial philosophy. CREEPS are not interested in developing future leaders because those individuals are viewed by CREEPS as threats. CREEPS love to show off their power.
- CREEPS are as *secretive* as possible. CREEPS don't like to share information with employees. Employees find out information through the grapevine. When CREEPS do have to share information with employees,

it is communicated through formal communication channels, and generally the employees are not allowed (or are only superficially allowed) to be
part of the decision-making process.

The difference between the right type of leader and CREEPS can also be
illustrated by slightly modifying the work of Peters and Austin (1985). Characteristics of the right type of leader include:

- Being comfortable with people
- Putting employees first
- Being an open-door cheerleader
- Not demanding a reserved parking place, private washroom, or dining
  room
- Having the common touch
- Being a good listener
- Being fair
- Being humble
- Being tough when confronting nasty problems
- Tolerating disagreement (respectful of the opinion of others)
- Having strong convictions (altruistic approach to life)
- Trusting people
- Giving credit, taking blame
- Preferring personal communication over such written communication as
  memos, e-mail, or long reports
- Keeping promises
- Thinking there are at least two other people in the organization who would
  be good administrators

The description of CREEPS is as follows:

- Being uncomfortable with people
- Putting their needs first, not the needs of the employees
- Being generally inaccessible to employees
- Having a reserved parking place, private washroom, and dining area
- Having a strained relationship with employees
- Being a good talker in terms of outlining what they want, being a poor
  listener
- Being fair to their favorite employees, exploiting the rest
- Being arrogant
- Avoiding nasty problems, being elusive, the artful dodger
- Not tolerating disagreement, not respecting the opinion of others
- Not having a firm stand, vacillating, and utilizing a Machiavellian ap-
  proach

- Distrusting employees and focusing upon numbers on reports
- Taking credit, blaming others for failures
- Preferring written communication over personal contact
- Not keeping promises
- Making sure that no one is hired who remotely resembles a qualified administrator (or a challenge to their authority)

In terms of organizational performance, which leadership style will achieve maximum performance? I think it is quite obvious that the right type of leader can create a workplace characterized by highly energized, dedicated, and productive employees always willing to do their best. A CREEPS leadership style will establish an organizational environment in which minimum performance is the norm.

An organization with the right type of leaders will outperform an organization filled with CREEPS because the right type of leaders can tap the full potential of the workforce. Thus, the first definitive key to organizational success and sustainability is to fill organizational leadership positions with the right type of leaders—meaning individuals who possess an altruistic approach to life and who focus upon the needs of the employees. CREEPS must be eliminated from leadership or managerial positions in order to maximize organizational performance.

The First Definite Key to Organizational Success and Sustainability

Fill organizational leadership positions with the right type of leaders—meaning individuals who possess the "right type of leader" characteristics described in the chapter. CREEPS must be eliminated from any leadership or managerial position in order to maximize organizational performance.

Figure 6.2.

Leadership and organizational success and sustainability are forever locked in an eternal struggle against the numerous forces that can devour an organization in today's highly competitive marketplace. The critical role of leadership can best be summarized by the following story that was told by Dr. Ronald Walker (2007) during a graduate class at Jackson State University:

> You can learn a lot about leadership by watching a farmer trying to get a group of cows to move from one pasture to another. The farmer can get behind the cows and try to push them through one gate and into another pasture. Eventually the farmer will get the cows into the other pasture; however, he would have spent a lot of time and used a lot of effort. Instead of trying to push the cows, the farmer could have observed which cow was the lead cow and placed a bucket of feed in front of that cow and easily, with minimum effort, led that

cow, and subsequently the other cows, out of one gate and through another
into a new pasture. However, what we must always be careful of is who has
the bucket and where are they leading us; it could be to the slaughterhouse.
(n.p.)

With the right type of leader, no one needs to worry about the direction in
which the organization is heading, for that decision would have been mutual-
ly agreed upon by management and the employees. Ultimately it is the values
and character of the right type of leader, which are grounded within an
altruistic approach to life, that foster the creation of a productive workplace
characterized by motivated employees who are always willing to do their
best. That is the kind of organization that will survive the rigors of the
marketplace and achieve sustainability.

In terms of education, each school needs the right type of leader, for it is
only those leaders who will create a school environment focused upon maximizing student learning and developing teachers so they can be the best they
can be, as the saying goes:

> Successful high schools are professional places for educators. In successful
> high schools, teachers feel like professionals. Successful schools are schools
> where teachers are treated as professionals, where teachers work in teams, and
> where professional development in the implementation of successful strategies
> is a common part of the experience of the professional educator. (Christensen,
> 2003, n.p.)

Having the right type of leader in every administrative position is the fifth
reality associated with education and learning.

CRITICAL POINTS TO REMEMBER

- The right type of leader can emerge only from an altruistic approach to
  life.
- The right type of leader focuses upon the needs of the employees, thereby
  creating a workplace characterized by highly motivated and productive
  employees who are focused upon satisfying the needs of the customer. In
  other words, the right type of leader pursues organizational goals and
  objectives in such a way that the growth and integrity of people are respected. Other characteristics of the right type of leader include being
  comfortable with people; putting employees first; being an open-door
  cheerleader; not demanding a reserved parking place, private washroom,
  or dining room; having the common touch; being a good listener; being
  fair; being humble; being tough when confronting nasty problems; tolerating disagreement (respectful of the opinion of others); having strong convictions (altruistic approach to life); trusting people; giving credit, taking

blame; preferring personal communication over such written communication as memos, e-mail, or long reports; keeping promises; and thinking there are at least two other people in the organization who would be good administrators.

• The fifth reality associated with education and learning is that the field of education needs the right type of leader in every administrative position—meaning individuals who possess the "right type of leader" characteristics described in the chapter. CREEPS must always be eliminated from any management or leadership position in order to maximize organizational performance and the learning environment.

REFERENCES

Christensen, D. (2003, September). Time to rethink the high school experience. *NCSA Today.* Retrieved http://www.nde.state.ne.us/COMMISH/HSexperience.htm, accessed January 29, 2008.

Gitman, L. J., & McDaniel, C. (2003). *The best of the future of business*. Mason, OH: Thomson/South-Western.

Hellriegel D., Slocum, J., and Woodman, R. (1995). *Organizational behavior*. 7th ed. St. Paul, MN: West Publishing.

Hill, C. W. L., & Jones, G. R. (1998). *Strategic management: An integrated approach*. Boston: Houghton Mifflin.

Interstate School Leaders Licensure Consortium of the Council of Chief State School Officers. (1997). *Candidate information bulletin for the school leaders licensure assessment*. Princeton, NJ: Educational Testing Service. The standards are available online at www.schoolbriefing.com/ISLLC-standards/.

Johnston, B. (1994). Educational administration in the postmodern age. In *Postmodern school leadership: Meeting the crisis in educational administration*, pp. 115–131, S. Maxcy (Ed.). Westport, CT: Praeger.

Levy, M. (2004). *Where else would you rather be?* Champaign, IL: Sports Publishing.

Moorhead, G., & Griffin, R. W. (1995). *Organizational behavior: Managing people and organizations*. 4th ed. Boston: Houghton Mifflin.

Peters, T., & Austin, N. (1985). *A passion for excellence*. New York: Random House.

Robbins, S. (2001). *Organizational behavior*. 9th ed. Upper Saddle River, NJ: Prentice-Hall.

Seyfarth, J. T. (1999). *The principal: New leadership for new challenges*. Upper Saddle River, NJ: Prentice-Hall.

Walker, R. (2007, Spring). Class lecture at Jackson State University.

Welch, J., & Welch, S. (2005, April 4). How to be a good leader. *Newsweek*, pp. 45–48.

Yulk, G., & Van Fleet, D. (1992). Theory and research on leadership in organizations. In *Handbook of industrial and organizational psychology*, vol. 3, pp. 147–198, M. D. Dunnette & L. M. Hough (Eds.). Palo Alto, CA: Consulting Psychologists Press.

Chapter Seven

The Finance Issue

We ought to finance the education of every child in America equitably.
—Jonathan Kozol (1991) cited in Brimley and Garfield (2008, p. 60)

When preparing mission statements, educational leaders must start with the reasons for the existence or purpose of a school. Once the purpose of the school has been clearly defined, a series of strategic goals is developed to accomplish the mission of the school. Objectives are then created to ensure that the goals are accomplished. Programs, services, and activities are designed around the objectives. Finally, human and financial resources are required so that programs, services, and activities can be offered. The bottom line is that human and financial resources play a critical factor in determining if the mission of a school is feasible.

A thorough examination of the financing of public education is beyond the scope of this book. As a consequence, a complete analysis of this issue is set aside. Instead, our journey is a straightforward movement toward the question, Does money matter?, and the sixth reality associated with education and learning.

EDUCATIONAL FINANCE INFORMATION (PROVIDED BY BRIMLEY & GARFIELD, 2008)

- Generally, property taxes are a major part of a local district's revenue, whereas sales and income taxes constitute the major source of state funds. (p. 95)
- Increases in educational spending are related to numerous variables: (1) changing enrollments of students; (2) additional programs and services

provided; (3) changing rates of inflation; and (4) inequities in the services provided among school districts. (p. 33)

- Seventy-five percent to 80% of total educational spending is for teachers' and administrative salaries. (p. 19)
- Eight hundred billion dollars was spent on public and private education from preprimary through graduate school. (p. 29)
- Annual spending per student nationally is $8,618. (p. 29)
- Percent distribution of revenue for public elementary and secondary schools (school year 2002–2003): state, 48.7%; local and intermediate, 42.8%; and federal, 8.5%. (p. 31)
- The average per-student expenditure among the states ranged from $5,245 in Utah to $15,073 in the District of Columbia between 2004 and 2005. (p. 30)

THE SIXTH REALITY OF EDUCATION AND LEARNING

The essence of the sixth reality regarding education and learning is illustrated by the following statement:

> Where children live has a powerful effect on the quality of the public schools they attend. Real estate agents are well acquainted with the question "How good are the public schools?" because parents who have the resources to do so shop for homes with the quality of local education in mind. Although public schools differ in many ways, one of the most important variables is per-pupil expenditure—the amount of money spent per student. Think of per-pupil expenditure as a financial package put together by local school boards with money received from the local, state, and federal governments. (Alexander & Salmon, 1995, cited in Newman, 2002, p. 347)

The sixth reality of education and learning is that per-pupil expenditure must be the same no matter where a student lives to ensure that each student has equal opportunities to learn.

The following statements are written by Joseph W. Newman (2002) and enforce the premise of the sixth truth of education and learning:

> Does money matter? To those who argue that money cannot buy everything, the best reply is that money can buy some things. To be sure, educators cannot correlate spending with achievement and promise more dollars will produce higher test scores. . . . What educators can state with confidence, though, is that educational programs and services do not come free. Only money can buy them. . . . In the wealthiest districts in a given state, high school students have access to a curriculum that offers five or six foreign languages, math and science courses through advanced calculus and second-year physics, challenging courses in other core subjects, and pupil–teacher ratios of 20 or 25 to 1. The cost may run to $15,000 or more per student. . . . The poorest districts

within a state offer their high school students a very different curriculum: one or two foreign languages, no calculus or physics, unexceptional courses in other subjects, and pupil–teacher ratios of 35 or 40 to 1. The price tag may be $5,000 or less per student. . . . People who believe money doesn't matter should tour schools as different as these. (p. 351)

Let's be clear: It is not about competition versus the traditional school system nor throwing more money at education; it is about equal funding. With equal funding it does not matter what school a student attends (traditional, charter, independent, and so forth) or where a student attends school because each student receives equal funding and equal opportunities to learn. Equal funding levels the playing field across the board. Students attending suburban schools, rural schools, or urban schools receive the same funding and should receive the same learning opportunities. Wealthier neighborhoods no longer have an advantage.

CRITICAL POINTS TO REMEMBER

• A society benefits when its citizens are educated. Providing quality education for all students benefits everyone in society. The short-run financial burden of providing quality education for all students will be paid for in the long run with increased productivity and higher standards of living.
• The sixth reality regarding education and learning is that per-pupil expenditure must be the same for every student to ensure that all students have equal opportunities to learn.

REFERENCES

Alexander, K., & Salmon, R. (1995). *Public school finance in the United States*. Needham, MA: Allyn & Bacon.

Brimley, V., & Garfield, R. (2008). *Financing education in a climate of change*. 10th ed. Boston: Allyn & Bacon/Pearson Education.

Kozol, J. (1991). *Savage inequalities*. New York: Harper Perennial.

Newman, J. (2002). *America's teachers: An introduction to education*. Boston: Allyn & Bacon/Pearson Education.

Chapter Eight

Not Everyone Needs to Go to College

The seventh reality regarding education and learning is that not everyone after completing high school needs to attend college.

—Daniel Wentland

The following statement reflects the myth regarding college and life:

In these days, it is doubtful that any child may reasonably be expected to succeed in life if he or she is denied the opportunity of a college education.

This statement has never been true in the past, present, or future. Reality is better reflected in the following statement by Murray (2008):

College professors commonly observe that students who come to college after a hitch in the military or after working for several years, paying their own tuition, tend to take their courses more seriously and have a clearer sense of why they are taking a course than students who have come straight from high school. (p. 101)

The ideology that everyone after finishing high school needs to go to college is simply a myth. As educational leaders and policymakers continue to chase the myth, a distortion is created in the marketplace for higher education. The market distortion results in higher tuition costs and enormous debt for students and parents. Myth chasing is never a good policymaking practice. Let's utilize supply and demand to illustrate the increase in tuition caused by the myth that everyone after completing high school needs to go to college (see figure 8.1).

Besides the increasing costs of a college education, by perpetuating the myth that everyone needs to go to college, students are being misled by the notion that a satisfying lifestyle cannot be achieved without college. There

45

College Tuition

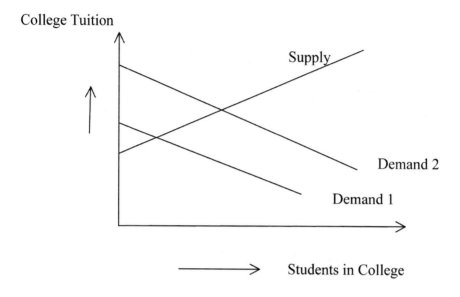

Figure 8.1. Supply and Demand

are plenty of opportunities to earn a comfortable living in retail, financial services, the building and trades industry, and so forth. By entering the workforce, individuals start to gain the experience and skills that will propel them up the career ladder without burdening themselves with the financial debt associated with college. There is nothing wrong with pursuing a technical education track in secondary education. Career and technical education (CTE) has helped many individuals obtain rewarding occupations.

Today there are 2,500 career academies in the United States serving the best and brightest students. The first was established in Philadelphia in 1965 and was designed to help students in low-income neighborhoods go to college and do well in their careers. Career academies are small schools within schools that are focused on career paths or themes. They allow students to specialize in career clusters, a term that includes health, communications, architecture, fine and performing arts, engineering, education, and agriculture. Companies and industries are closely tied to these programs, offering apprenticeships, job shadowing, and mentoring.

The goal of CTE is not to steer kids away from college but to provide an opportunity to enter the workforce to gain valuable knowledge, skills, and abilities that will make an individual more productive and better prepared for college or a professional trade school or association. Today, CTE programs basically blur the lines between college preparation programs and career preparation programs.

THE RACE ISSUE

Individuals who bring race into every topic and try to pit one segment of society against another (the divide-and-conquer strategy) need to open their minds and move away from the ideology that not having everyone attend college is race related. The reason is straightforward; the reality of not attending college immediately after graduating from high school applies to individuals of every race. Many entrepreneurs, trade persons, self-made individuals, and high school graduates who have decided to enter the workforce instead of attending college have gone on to achieve a successful and rewarding life, and that success applies to members of every race. Every day there are stories in newspapers or broadcast on television programs that highlight individuals who have accomplished amazing things in life without immediately entering college after high school. College is only one path to possibly achieving satisfaction in life. For many individuals, attending college immediately after high school was a disastrous decision that led to financial ruin and emotional trauma. By the way, the reality that not everyone needs to go to college after graduating from high school does not imply that an individual will not attend college later in life when he or she is better prepared emotionally, intellectually, and financially for the rigors of the higher-education learning environment.

CRITICAL POINTS TO REMEMBER

- Sanoff (2006, p. B9) states, "Many college faculty members comment that their students are ill prepared for the demands of higher education."
- Perpetuating the myth that everyone after completing high school needs to attend college has resulted in students incurring enormous amounts of debt and the misperception that a satisfying life cannot be achieved without college. The seventh reality regarding education and learning is that not everyone after finishing high school needs to go to college.

REFERENCES

Murray, C. (2008). *Real education: Four simple truths for bringing America's schools back to reality.* New York: Crown Forum/Random House.

Sanoff, A. (2006, March 10). A perception gap over students' preparation. *The Chronicle of Higher Education*, pp. B9–B14. Retrieved September 20, 2006, from EBSCO host research database.

Chapter Nine

Streamlining the P–16 Academic Pipeline

The new National Assessment of Educational Progress (NAEP) report comes as colleges and employers are complaining that too many students earn diplomas without learning the skills needed for college or the workplace.
—Robert Tomsho (2009, p. A5)

A major problem in the educational pipeline is the substantial gap between what students do in high school and what they are expected to do in college (Cooper, Chavira, & Mena, 2005; Venezia, Kirst, & Antonio, 2003). The following statistics illustrate the lack of college preparedness (Borja, 2006; Kirst & Venezia, 2001; McCarthy & Kuh, 2006):

- Of the students who do not complete high school on time, only 27% of the original group of ninth-graders make it to the second year of college.
- Three fifths of students in two-year colleges and one fourth in four-year institutions require one or more years of remedial coursework.
- More than one fourth of four-year college students who require three or more remedial classes drop out of college after the first year.
- Graduation rates at the least-selective public universities in many states range between 30% and 50%.

These statistics represent only the tip of the iceberg relating to the disconnect between the elementary and secondary portion of the educational pipeline (pre-kindergarten through high school) and the higher-education segment. Taken in its entirety, the educational pipeline is abbreviated by P–16 and represents the entire educational process that a student must complete to obtain an undergraduate degree.

49

It is not only student achievement that is directly impacted by the breakdown between the segments of the educational pipeline; the competitiveness of the United States is also threatened. Naik (2006) reports that China's massive investment in education has been bearing fruit: "China is increasingly making its mark with scientific discoveries and patents held by scientists" (p. A2). Naik further mentions that even though the United States remains a research and development powerhouse, investment by other countries in education and research and development represents a constant challenge to the United States and its productivity rate and the standard of living currently enjoyed by U.S. citizens. Any course in economics will demonstrate the clear link between increases in productivity and an improvement in the quality of life. Productivity is the key to economic success, and education is a factor that impacts productivity.

P–16 EDUCATIONAL FACTS

The National Center for Education Statistics (NCES) reported in 2006 that the average high school graduation rate was 73.9% and that on average only 20 out of any 100 ninth-graders graduate with an associate's degree within three years or a bachelor's within six years (Borja, 2006). Additional statistics (Kirst & Venezia, 2001; McCarthy & Kuh, 2006; Olson, 2006b) indicate a breakdown in the educational pipeline:

- Almost four fifths (78%) of students in career/vocational courses planning on going to college were not taking college-preparation courses.
- Twenty-two percent of first-year college students require remediation in math.
- Seventy-eight percent of seniors wrote three or fewer papers or reports of more than five pages in length.
- Just over six in ten students earn an undergraduate degree within six years. The figures are worse for poor, minority, and first-generation college students.
- More than one quarter of freshmen at four-year colleges and nearly half of those at two-year colleges do not make it to their second year.

Beneath these statistics are several issues impacting student readiness for college, the first being a lack of early and high-quality counseling for many students (Kirst & Venezia, 2001). The U.S. Department of Education recommends a high school student-to-counselor ratio of 250 to 1, however the national average is 284 to 1 (Borja, 2006). With such high ratios, the overall effectiveness of counseling has to be questioned.

A second issue is the lack of communication provided to students and parents regarding supplementary academic services. David Hoff (2006) reports that under No Child Left Behind (NCLB), schools that fail to meet achievement targets for three consecutive years must offer tutoring and other extended learning programs to all students. Hoff further states that the Government Accountability Office estimated that only 19% of eligible students used the supplementary services in the 2004–2005 school year. There needs to be more effort to promote the availability of these supplementary programs to students and their parents.

A third issue is the dilemma that there are multiple definitions of what is meant by high school student readiness for college (Olson, 2006b). For example, should high school students who have successfully completed a college-preparatory curriculum be considered ready to succeed at college? Or should student readiness for college be defined as scores on admissions or placement tests or grades earned in high school (Olson, 2006b)? Olson further suggests other possible definitions or measurements of student readiness, including: (a) skills and knowledge college professors view as needed to do credit-bearing work or (b) the lack of needing remedial coursework.

A fourth issue is that high school performance expectations are far short of what students need to succeed in college. The following statistics (Kirst & Venezia, 2006; McCarthy & Kuh, 2006; Olson, 2001) illustrate the level of student unpreparedness for college:

- Forty-seven percent of high school students stated they spent three or fewer hours per week studying. First-year students at four-year colleges spend twice as many hours per week studying, while at community college, 25% of students stated that they spent 11 or more hours a week studying.
- While more than 7 in 10 recent high school graduates enroll in higher education, nearly half of all college students take at least one remedial course, and more than one quarter of freshmen at four-year colleges and nearly half of those at a community college do not make it to the sophomore year.
- Even though high school students spent little time studying, four fifths stated that they often or very often come to class with completed assignments.
- Only about 51% stated that they were challenged to do their best work in school.
- Only 35% were excited about their classes.
- How does this mediocre overall level of effort translate into grades? About 45% who spent three hours or less a week preparing for class received As or Bs.

- Four fifths (80%) of high school students spend three hours or less a week reading assigned material. Seventeen percent of seniors stated that they did not have to spend any time on assigned material.
- Less than one fifth of ninth-graders who finish high school within four years go to college and complete a bachelor's degree within six years.

Clearly the statistics indicate that many high school students spend a modest amount of time studying, devote little effort to reading and writing, and take too few math classes (McCarthy & Kuh, 2006). "When students take Algebra 1, Algebra 2, and geometry courses in high school, why aren't they ready for a college algebra course?" (Schmeiser cited in Olson, 2006b, pp. 1, 26, 28-29).

In a statement titled "With Renewed Hope and Determination," a group of 18 higher-education leaders, mostly university presidents and chancellors, joined with 10 district superintendents and said the following:

> Our nation is no longer well served by an education system that prepares a few to attend college to develop their minds for learned pursuits while the rest are expected only to build their muscles for useful labor. In the 21st century, all students must meet higher achievement standards in elementary, secondary, and post-secondary schools and thus be better prepared to meet the challenges of work and citizenship. (Chenoweth, 2000, p. 14)

All too often the high school curriculum does not align with community college or university requirements, and far too many students have to take remediation classes; ultimately, the losers are the students (Finkel, 2007). According to a recent study, "41% of entering community college students and 29% of all entering college students are underprepared in at least one of the basic skills, reading, writing, and math" (Byrd & MacDonald, 2005, p. 22).

Obviously, much work needs to be done in terms of developing a seamless transition between each segment in the educational pipeline. "We must harmonize what high schools expect of their graduates with what universities expect of their freshmen" (Finn, 2006, p. B40).

RECOMMENDATIONS

What can be done to reverse the lack of student readiness for college? First, there needs to be more collaboration between the secondary and higher-education portions of the educational pipeline (Gilroy, 2003; Kirst & Venezia, 2001; Sewall, 1999). "Calling the relationship between K–12 and higher education 'dysfunctional,' a group of policymakers has called for more collaboration between the two systems, specifically identifying cooperation in the areas of raising academic standards, teacher preparation, and community involvement as being critical to improving education in the United States" (Gilroy, 2003, p. 19). Keller (2006) cites an example where North Carolina Central University in Durham teamed up with Southern High School, a low-performing school in the Durham School District, to teach students math and sciences courses. Officials from Durham School District and the university stated that there are advantages all around when the secondary and higher-education segments of the academic pipeline work collaboratively for the benefit of the students.

Second, states must begin to adopt standards and tests with college success in mind (Olson, 2001). "We must make sure that there is consistency between what students are being required to do in order to graduate from high school and higher-education admission requirements," states Judith I. Gill, Massachusetts's higher-education chancellor (Olson, 2001). A growing number of states, policymakers, and other community leaders are attempting to link high school course requirements with college-level comprehension requirements.

In 1999, at a national education summit, governors and corporate leaders agreed that states should move to align higher-education admission standards with high school graduation requirements and reduce or eventually phase out remediation at college institutions (Olson, 2001). In another national education summit in 2005, state governors agreed on a broad set of actions viewed as necessary to close the academic gap between the high school and higher-education segments of the educational pipeline. The actions included: (a) raising graduation requirements and academic standards, (b) building stronger data and measurement systems, (c) better preparing teachers, (d) redesigning high schools structurally and academically, and (e) holding K–12 and postsecondary systems accountable for results (Olson, 2006a).

A third recommendation is that the community college system needs to better align its curriculum with the university system so that students have the knowledge and skills to succeed in upper-level courses. Just like the P–12 educational system needs to better prepare students for entry into the higher–education segment, community colleges need to ensure that course content meets the requirements for students to be successful in advanced courses offered in the junior and senior years at the university level.

A fourth recommendation focuses upon specific activities that high schools can perform to help improve student performance. These activities include, but are not limited to: (a) peer-tutoring programs, (b) a homework hotline manned by volunteer teachers and honor roll students, (c) quizzes on homework, (d) periodic bonus questions on assigned readings, (e) homeroom extended 10 minutes in order to conduct a 20-minute schoolwide reading period implemented each morning, (f) increasing the number of required reading and writing assignments, and (g) recruiting parents and volunteers to help teachers with routine paperwork and other activities so teachers could provide prompt and helpful feedback to students on written assignments (McCarthy & Kuh, 2006).

A fifth recommendation suggested by Venezia, Kirst, and Antonio (2003) is to expand dual or concurrent enrollment programs between high schools and institutions of higher education. Venezia, Kirst, and Antonio further suggest that federal and state grants should be expanded to stimulate more K–16 policymaking. Specifically, federal and state grants should be available for: (a) collaborative discussions between K–12 and postsecondary education in an attempt to improve collection and use of data across the systems and (b) joint development activities that enable students to transition successfully from one segment of the educational pipeline to another.

A sixth recommendation is to develop programs aimed at incoming ninth-graders so that these students can receive the counseling and academic support necessary to succeed in school. Kirst and Venezia (2006) state, "Our education system is letting too many young people fall through the cracks" (p. B36).

A seventh and final recommendation is that states must do a better job of recruiting quality teachers for inner-city and rural schools (Caboni & Adisu, 2004). The quality of the teacher in the classroom has ramifications for the learning environment. The federal and state governments need to actively promote teaching as a worthy profession and provide the necessary funding to attract quality individuals to the field.

In conclusion, the information in this chapter illustrates that a problem in one sector of the educational pipeline impacts the entire educational system, and in many cases the problem cannot be solved without the cooperation of the other sectors. The fact that there are breakdowns within the educational pipeline where students are not being successfully transitioned along the P–16 pipeline constitutes the eighth reality associated with education and learning.

CRITICAL POINTS TO REMEMBER

- The breakdown between the segments within the educational pipeline not only threatens student achievement, but the competitiveness of the United States is also jeopardized. Cited in a 2007 report published by the World Economic Forum, the United States was rated the most competitive economy in the world, followed by Switzerland, Denmark, Sweden, Germany, Finland, and Singapore. "Today one-third of the world's science and engineering graduates are employed in the United States, and the United States accounts for 40 percent of the world's research and development expenditure" (Scherer, 2006/2007, p. 7). However, investments by other countries in education and research and development represent a constant challenge to the United States and the standard of living currently enjoyed by U.S. citizens. The established body of knowledge in economics clearly demonstrates the direct link between increases in productivity and the quality of life enjoyed by the citizens of a country. In sum, the key to economic success is productivity, and education is a factor impacting productivity.

- Given the link between productivity and the need for a highly educated and skilled workforce in today's global economy, the best minds in research and development must work alongside educational practitioners in an effort to learn how to effectively educate all students in a full range of subject areas, across all grade levels, and to capture that knowledge in replicable and scalable forms (Donovan, 2009).
- Each segment of the P–16 academic pipeline should provide students with the building blocks to succeed at the next educational level. Unfortunately the eighth reality regarding education and learning is that there are leaks within the P–16 academic pipeline where students are not being successfully transitioned from one segment of the P–16 pipeline to the next.

REFERENCES

Borja, R. (2006, September 27). College-counseling effort blends public, private resources. *Education Week*, p. 7.

Byrd, K., & MacDonald, G. (2005, Fall). Defining college readiness from the inside out: First generation college student perspectives. *Community College Review*, 33(1), pp. 22–37.

Caboni, T. C., & Adisu, M. (2004). A nation at risk after 20 years: Continuing implications for higher education. [Electronic version]. *Peabody Journal of Education*, 79(1), pp. 164–176.

Chenoweth, K. (2000, January 1). Thinking K–16. *Black issues in higher education*, 16(23), pp. 14–17. Retrieved October 6, 2006, from EBSCO host research database.

Cooper, C. R., Chavira, G., & Mena, D. D. (2005). From pipelines to partnerships: A synthesis of research on how diverse families, schools, and communities support children's pathways through school. [Electronic version]. *Journal of Education for Students Placed at Risk*, 10(4), pp. 407–430.

Donovan, S. (2009, February 11). Building "institutional infrastructure" and building research into the classroom. *Education Week*, pp. 24–25.

Finkel, E. (2007). Study: Testing at California high schools, community colleges misaligned. *Community College Week*, 19(24), pp. 7–8.

Finn, Jr., C. (2006). Obstacles on the route from high school to college. *Chronicle of Higher Education*, 52(27), pp. B40–B42.

Gilroy, M. (2003, March). Articulating the K–16 dream. *Education Digest*, 68(7), pp. 19–25. Retrieved October 6, 2006, from EBSCO host research database.

Hoff, D. J. (2006, September 27). House panel studies ways to boost tutoring under NCLB. *Education Week*, p. 23.

Keller, B. (2006, October 4). N.C. university faculty bail out high school in math, science class. *Education Week*, p. 14.

Kirst, M., & Venezia, A. (2001, September). Bridging the great divide between secondary and postsecondary education. [Electronic version]. *Phi Delta Kappan*, 83(1), pp. 92–98.

Kirst, M., & Venezia, A. (2006, March 10). What states must do. *Chronicle of Higher Education*, pp. B36–B37. Retrieved October 12, 2006, from EBSCO host research database.

McCarthy, M., & Kuh, G. D. (2006, May). Are the students ready for college? What student engagement data say. [Electronic version]. *Phi Delta Kappan*, 87(9), pp. 664–669.

Naik, G. (2006, September 29). China's spending for research outpaces the U.S. *Wall Street Journal*, pp. A2, A4.

Olson, L. (2001, May 9). K–12 and college expectations often fail to mesh. *Education Week*, 20(34), pp. 1–6. Retrieved October 6, 2006, from EBSCO host research database.

Olson, L. (2006a, February 22). States acting to raise bar on H.S. skills. *Education Week*, 25(24), pp. 1, 20-21. Retrieved October 6, 2006, from EBSCO host research database.

Olson, L. (2006b, April 26). Views differ on defining college prep. *Education Week*, 25(33), pp. 1, 26, 28-29. Retrieved October 6, 2006, from EBSCO host research database.

Scherer, M. (2006, December/2007, January). Happiness vs. achievement? *Educational Leadership*, 64(4), p. 7.

Sewall, A. M. (1999, Winter). New frames for an undefined future. *National Forum*, 79(1), pp. 3–5. Retrieved October 6, 2006, from EBSCO host research database.

Tomsho, R. (2009, April 29). Few gains are seen in high school test. *Wall Street Journal*, p. A5.

Venezia, A., Kirst, M. W., & Antonio, A. L. (2003, May). Fix K–16 disconnections, or betray the college dream. *Education Digest*, 68(9), pp. 34–40. Retrieved October 12, 2006, from EBSCO host research database.

World Economic Forum (2007–2008). *The Global Competitiveness Report*. New York: Palgrave Macmillan.

Chapter Ten

Is It Hopeless?

Public education is a political activity; as such, it is a fertile arena for conflict. Conflict provides opportunity to examine, clarify, and compare the mission (purpose and function) of the school with the wants and needs of the society it serves.

—Norton, Webb, Dlugosh, and Sybouts (1996, p. 101)

Have you ever worked for an organization where it felt as if no one cared about you and that your contribution to the organization was always minimized? Unfortunately, I have worked for several organizations like that, with the worst being a situation where senior officials thought they were the greatest things on earth and the rest of us were there to do their bidding. The message emanating throughout that institution consisted of fear and intimidation. Each employee dreaded every workday, and very few employees went beyond what was required to do their jobs. Just trying to make it to Friday was the fuel that kept us going.

Gaining an insight into the dynamics within an organization is an endeavor that has its roots embedded in systems theory. A *system* is a group of interrelated or interacting elements forming a unified whole that works toward a common goal by accepting inputs and producing outputs in an organized transformation process. A dynamic system essentially has three basic interacting components or functions: (1) an input function that involves capturing and assembling elements that enter the system to be processed, (2) a processing element or transformation process that converts an input into an output, and (3) the output that has been produced. A cybernetic system includes two additional components: (1) feedback and (2) control. *Feedback* is the data about the performance of a system. *Control* involves monitoring and evaluating feedback to determine whether a system is moving toward the achievement of its goal(s). In addition, a system can either be classified as an

57

open system or an adaptive system. An *open system* is a system that interacts with other systems in its environment. An *adaptive system* has the ability to change itself or its environment in order to survive.

Every organization has all three components: input, processing, and output. An effective and efficient organization has all five system components working together as a harmonious whole—these three, as well as feedback and control. Thus, systems theory provides a meaningful methodology for examining the workings of an organization as it interacts with other organizations.

Another framework for conceptualizing what constitutes a system is provided by Patrick Morley in his book *Coming Back to God*: "The 'collection' of ideas we embrace forms a system that guides our choices, and hence shapes the course of our future. Here's the problem: If the 'system' you build will not work, you will not know it doesn't work for ten or twenty years. By then, damage is done and you will have given the best years of your life to a system that has failed you" (Morley, 2001, p. 20).

Morley's main point is that the system that has been established was designed to produce the results or outcomes that are occurring, whether those outcomes are positive or negative. From an organizational perspective, what can be learned from Morley's ideas? The ramifications are quite clear: If your organization is underperforming, it is *the systems that have been established within the organization that are producing those poor results*. To correct the situation, those systems must be either modified or abandoned (in which case, new systems will need to be developed).

Public education is a social/political system established to deliver good education to the students who attend it (Levine, 1971). A political system is a mechanism through which societal values are debated, assigned a sense of importance, and converted into public policy (Norton, Webb, Dlugosh, & Sybouts, 1996). Four factors that affect the distribution of values by policymakers include: (1) quality, (2) efficiency, (3) equity, and (4) choice (decision making). As outlined by Norton, Webb, Dlugosh, and Sybouts (1996), quality issues are concerned with establishing "standards aimed to produce substantial improvements for those for whom the policy is designed" (p. 93). Efficiency is concerned with minimizing costs while maximizing gains, outcomes, or product. Equity deals with redistribution of resources to provide relief for or satisfaction of a human need. Finally, policymakers must make a decision whether to adopt or reject a policy. These four factors (quality, efficiency, equity, and choice) eventually manifest themselves in statutes and can lead to conflict in the political arena (Norton, Webb, Dlugosh, & Sybouts, 1996, pp. 92–93).

Public education, like any social/political system, has its share of conflicts and problems, including improving graduation rates; reducing dropout rates; closing the achievement gap between white and minority, low-income, disabled, and non-English students; reducing funding inequities between school districts; attracting and retaining qualified teachers, especially in low-income districts; and designing a curriculum (Brimley & Garfield, 2008, p. 35). Are these educational problems insurmountable? No, there is hope. The realities associated with education and learning provide the clarity that has been missing in the field of education. It is like adjusting the lens on a microscope so you can focus upon what is being studied. What was once blurry can now be clearly seen. As we move into the final section of the book, we sharpen the picture to see how to improve the educational environment.

CRITICAL POINTS TO REMEMBER

- Public education is a social/political system established to deliver good education to the students who attend it.
- Public education, like any social/political system, has its share of conflicts and problems.
- The national debate over education is not just about the end product, but equally important, it is over the means—"curriculum, pedagogy, and assessment—and where the emphasis on content and skill acquisition and its measurement ought to be placed, given limited time and resources" (Hersh, 2009, p. 28).
- Are educational problems insurmountable? No, there is hope. The realities associated with education and learning provide a pathway from which the problems associated with education and learning can be clearly examined.

REFERENCES

Brimley, V., & Garfield, R. (2008). *Financing education in a climate of change.* 10th ed. Boston: Allyn & Bacon/Pearson Education.

Hersh, R. (2009, April 22). Our 21st-century "risk": Teaching for content *and* skills. *Education Week,* pp. 28–29.

Levine, D. V. (1971). Concepts of bureaucracy in urban school reform. *Phi Delta Kappan,* 52, pp. 329–333. Reprinted in Kretovics, J., & Nussel, E., Eds. (1994). *Transforming urban education,* pp. 99-108. Boston: Allyn & Bacon.

Morley, P. (2001). *Coming back to God.* Grand Rapids, MI: Zondervan Publishing House.

Norton, M. S., Webb, L. D., Dlugosh, L., & Sybouts, W. (1996). *The school superintendency: New responsibilities, new leadership.* Upper Saddle River, NJ: Allyn & Bacon.

II

Given Reality, How Can Education Be Improved?

Chapter Eleven

The First Step

> At a certain point there were just so many mixed messages and contradictory directives and policies that we didn't really know what to do.
>
> —Kevin Clark (2009, p. 42)

Politicians, economists, business executives, educators, and just about everyone else make the claim that education is important, so if education is so important, what exactly is it? Unfortunately a straightforward definition has proven elusive because education has been described in numerous ways by many individuals:

- "Throughout history, organized education has served many purposes—the transmission of tradition, knowledge, skills; the acculturation and socialization of the young; the building and preserving of political-economic systems; the provision of opportunity for social mobility; the enhancement of the quality of life; and the cultivation of individual potential, among others" (Noll, 2008, p. 2).
- "The aim of an educational system is the same in every age and in every society where such a system can exist: it is to improve man as man" (Hutchins, 1953, cited in Noll, 2008, p. 11).
- "Some schools give all their energy to boosting the ~~~~nce of their lowest achievers. Others aim to challenge only the ~ est potential. Still others are intent on increasing t on the tests they give students" (Scherer, 2008, p. 7
- "Education's highest aim is to create moral and (Haynes, 2009, p. 6).
- "Education . . . is responsible for the encultura preparation of the young for citizenship and w gosh, & Sybouts, 1996, p. 87).

63

- "Schools should encourage the development of all aspects of whole persons: their intellectual, moral, social, aesthetic, emotional, physical, and spiritual capacities" (Noddings, 2008, p. 9).
- "The uniform objectives of basic schooling should be threefold. . . . Our society provides all children ample opportunity. . . . All the children will become, when of age, full-fledged citizens with suffrage and other political responsibilities. . . . When they are grown, all (or certainly most) of the children will engage in some form of work to earn a living" (Adler, 1982, cited in Noll, 2008, pp. 18–19).

The confusion continues:

- "All societies have a compelling interest in building school systems whose graduates are prepared for a diverse global workplace" (Scherer, 2007, p. 7).
- "Do changing demographics in society mean we should rethink U.S. public education? If so, what should schools do differently? . . . Educational policymakers should not necessarily redesign education to suit changing demographics. Instead, we need to ensure once and for all that every child attends a school with strong academic programs, qualified and motivated teachers, and a respectful and nurturing environment" (Wadsworth & Remaley, 2007, p. 23).
- "One of the most serious challenges facing educational leaders is to gain a community consensus on what the expectations are for schools" (Gallagher, Bagin, & Moore, 2005, p. 4).
- "Schools across the world—whether in Africa, the Americas, Asia, Europe, or Oceania—tend to share some basic features: they are designed to prepare children and youth to become engaged citizens, ethical human beings, and productive workers who will contribute to the societies in which they live" (Suarez-Orozco & Sattin, 2007, p. 58).
- "The dilemma between equity—the belief in equal education for all children, regardless of the disadvantages or disabilities they bring to school—and excellence—the need for all children to reach high standards—caused tension and conflict in public debate" (Sergiovanni, Kelleher, McCarthy, & Wirt, 2004, p. 212).
- "What is the aim of education? Is the primary goal of schooling to train young people to pass tests and get good grades, or is it, as Jean Piaget once put it, 'To train young people to think for themselves and not to accept the first idea that comes to them'" (Elkind, 2006, p. vii).

he list can go on and on, seemingly stretching to infinity, where, de- who is asked, the definition and purpose of education can take on an array of answers, just like the numerous descriptions that eyewitnesses provide when describing what occurred during the commission of a crime.

The confusion over the role of education reminds me of a company scrambling to find its identity in the marketplace. In fact, the business landscape is littered with examples of corporations that have failed to maximize stakeholder value because they lost their direction or drifted into all sorts of business ventures without first acquiring the knowledge and expertise to manage those ventures.

A classic example is Sears, which in 1981 expanded into real estate and financial services, only to experience a decline in its core business of retailing. By 1993, Sears had sold all its financial units, yet it continued to experience sales and image problems in its retailing division. Sears has still not recovered from its management team's misadventure into uncharted waters (where Sears had limited or no experience). The company's series of missteps culminated when Kmart took over Sears in November 2004. The once-powerful number-one retailer in the nation was reduced to the status of takeover victim and is now playing a secondary role to another struggling retail company. The lesson to be learned is that poor managerial decisions can cause a company to lose its identity, resulting in an overall lack of direction and purpose that eventually diverts and dilutes the human resource capabilities of an organization. Sears was a major retailer, but when it lost its focus on retail, its financial performance eroded.

What happened to Sears is what is occurring today with education. Educational performance is diminishing because of a lack of focus. Educational practitioners, policymakers, and scholars go round and round regarding the "business of education" just like a merry-go-round. Up and down the wooden horses go, but the ride begins and ends exactly where it started. The educational merry-go-round will never end until all the proposed definitions and purposes of education are woven together by a common thread that can act as a starting point from which all educational analysis can flow.

Without a common thread, or starting point, chaos and confusion trump order and impede progress toward uncovering academic truths. For example, in economics the starting point is the notion of scarcity—unlimited wants for goods and services versus limited resources. From that starting point, economists have plotted a steady course of discovery culminating in the economic way of thinking. To master economics, students must understand and model the economic way of thinking. The economic way of thinking is the path upon which one can understand the world.

So what can serve as the starting point or common thread in education? Quite simply, the "business of education" is all about learning, with learning being defined as acquiring new knowledge, skills, and/or abilities. Every task, practice, procedure, financial decision, theory or model, research effort, educational proposal, and organizational analysis must be anchored by the understanding that the field of education exists solely for the purpose of understanding and promoting learning. Many in education understand this, but many have forgotten or become lost in a forest of ludicrous educational philosophies, and certainly many stakeholders have numerous other educational and political agendas.

By clarifying the purpose or mission of education and specifically defining learning as acquiring new knowledge, skills, and/or abilities, the confusing array of educational objectives captured in the second reality of education and learning is swept away. Clearing the educational landscape of the clutter that has been built up over the years is the first crucial step toward improving the educational environment. Divisive political ideologies and superficial educational issues are pushed to the side. With a unified mission and a clear definition of learning, the goal of improving education can move forward. Educational improvement now becomes a straightforward process. Any proposed solution for improving education (1) must be grounded in the mission of education, meaning understanding and promoting learning, no other social agendas, and (2) must flow from the realities associated with education and learning because the educational environment is governed by those realities. Ignoring this truth is like ignoring the fact that gravity is the underlying force of the universe. Ignoring reality will never lead to anything positive. The choice is to accept reality or continue down the messy path that so characterizes the world of education today.

THE EDUCATION AND LEARNING CYCLE

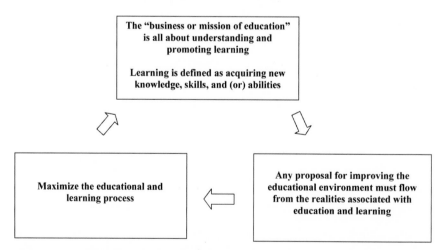

Figure 11.1.   Education and Learning Cycle

Everything in life, whether natural or manmade, has a beginning and an ending. In terms of improving education and learning, everything starts and ends with the realities associated with education and learning. Gaining a further understanding of the education and learning cycle is the path that we must now follow.

CRITICAL POINTS TO REMEMBER

• For too long the field of education has been drifting from fad to fad in the hope of improving the learning process; this endless game of wasting scarce resources and moving full speed toward nowhere must end.
• To end the game, the various definitions and proposed purposes of education that have been suggested over the years by so many individuals need to be set aside along with the various political agendas and ideologies that have dominated the field of education. The "business or mission of education" is about one thing: understanding and promoting learning.
• Learning is defined as acquiring new knowledge, skills, and/or abilities—period.
• With one purpose or mission for education and one definition of learning, the process of improving education becomes straightforward and is summarized by the education and learning cycle.

REFERENCES

Adler, M. (1982, July). The Paideia proposal: Rediscovering the essence of education. *American School Board Journal*.

Clark, K. (2009, April). The case for structured English immersion. *Educational Leadership* (66)7, p. 42.

Elkind, D. (2006). Foreword, pp. vii–ix. In Armstrong, T. *The best schools*. Alexandria, VA: Association for Supervision and Curriculum Development.

Gallagher, D., Bagin, D., & Moore, E. (2005). *The school and community relations*. 8th ed. Boston: Allyn & Bacon.

Haynes, C. (2009, May). Schools of conscience. *Educational Leadership*, (66)8, p. 6.

Hutchins, R. (1953). *The conflict in education in a democratic society*. New York: Harper & Row; renewed in 1981 by V. S. Hutchins.

Noddings, N. (2008, February). All our students thinking. *Educational Leadership*, (65)5, p. 9.

Noll, J. (2008). *Taking sides: Clashing views on educational issues*. 14th ed. Dubuque, IA: McGraw-Hill.

Norton, M. S., Webb, L. D., Dlugosh, L., & Sybouts, W. (1996). *The school superintendency: New responsibilities, new leadership*. Upper Saddle River, NJ: Allyn & Bacon.

Scherer, M. (2007, March). Hot-button issue. *Educational Leadership*, 64(6), p. 7.

Scherer, M. (2008, October). The question of excellence. *Educational Leadership*, 66(2), p. 7.

Sergiovanni, T., Kelleher, P., McCarthy, M., & Wirt, F. (2004). *Educational governance and administration*. 5th ed. Boston: Pearson Education, Allyn & Bacon.

Suarez-Orozco, M., & Sattin, C. (2007, April). Wanted: global citizens. *Educational Leadership*, (64)7, p. 58.

Wadsworth, D., & Remaley, M. (2007, March). What families want. *Educational Leadership*, (64)6, p. 23.

Chapter Twelve

The Structural Environment of Education

People respond to what is around them.

—Philip Crosby (1989, p. 179)

A student's life can be transformed by the school that he attends. For our purposes, the structural environment of education refers to the variables under the control or influence of a school. The key structural characteristics that impact learning include: (a) the leadership at a school, (b) the school's culture, (c) the classroom environment, and (d) the facilities in which the learning process takes place.

EDUCATIONAL LEADERSHIP

Educational leaders can establish an environment that will have a profound influence upon learning. Effective educational leadership can be illustrated by six comprehensive standards: (1) a vision of learning; (2) a culture of teaching and learning; (3) the management of learning; (4) relationships with the broader community to foster learning; (5) integrity, fairness, and ethics in learning; and (6) the political, social, economic, legal, and cultural context of learning (Johnson, 2005; see table 12.1).

THE INFLUENCE OF A SCHOOL'S CULTURE

Gaining an insight into the dynamics within an organization and realizing that organizational culture can positively or negatively impact organizational performance is nothing new; in fact, it can be traced back to the concept of

Characteristics of Effective Educational Leaders	
Vision of Learning	Stresses a continuous focus on understanding and promoting learning.
Culture of Teaching and Learning	Values and respects students, teachers, and staff members.
The management of the learning process	Includes several principles: (a) establishing effective and efficient operational procedures, (b) prioritizing and choosing programs and strategies that are most likely to stimulate learning, (c) understanding the nuances of federal, state, and district funding mechanisms, (d) employing teacher recruitment and selection strategies, and (e) encouraging teacher growth and development while removing poor performing teachers.
Relationships with the broader community to foster learning	Creates an educational environment where parents and other community stakeholders feel valued, welcome, and respected. Works with educational personnel throughout the P-16 academic pipeline to ensure that students are prepared to advance to the next academic level.
Integrity, fairness, and ethics in learning	Acts with integrity, fairness, and in an ethical manner.
The political, social, economic, legal, and cultural context of learning	Responds to, skillfully negotiates, and attempts to influence the larger political, social, economic, legal, and cultural environments that influence the educational environment.

Table 12.1: Characteristics of Effective Educational Leaders

institutionalization, whereby an organization takes on a life of its own well beyond the original vision of the founder(s). The management and educational leadership literature contains many descriptive characterizations of organizational culture that illustrate the positive and negative aspects of an organization's culture. However, what is missing in most of the educational leadership research is a specific measurement of the relationship between the academic excellence of a school and its culture.

To assess the culture of a school and its impact on academic excellence, we identify three workplace parameters that form the boundaries for four specific school cultures. These four school cultures, in turn, set the stage for the development of our School Excellence Model of Organizational Culture (SEMOC). This model provides a unique vision for predicting the academic excellence of a school based on its culture, with the objective of developing a course of action to improve the school's culture and, more importantly, the academic quality of the school.

Once the model is explained, we highlight the connection between the SEMOC and the "people factor" within an organization. Ultimately, it is the quality of the employees within an organization that determines the fate of an organization. An organization's employees have always made the difference between a truly successful organization and a mediocre entity. The primary driving force that brings people into a concert hall is to hear enchanting music performed by trained musicians whose skills and talents are on display. Highly qualified employees produce quality outputs and provide quality service that satisfies consumer needs. Highly skilled and trained teachers, administrators, and support staff set the stage for a quality educational experience. My premise here is that schools with cultures that focus on their people and that invest in their future will, in the long run, achieve a higher level of academic excellence than school cultures that view employees as mere costs to be reduced in times of trouble.

In the world of business, the Wegmans chain of grocery stores, headquartered in Rochester, New York, has repeatedly been cited as one of the best employers in the United States to work for. The company's focus on its employees has made Wegmans a shining example of a local, family-managed organization that can effectively and efficiently compete against national and international grocery chains. At this point, let us provide a better explanation of organizational structure, design, and culture.

Organizational Structure, Design, and Culture

In 1832, Charles Babbage suggested that the scientific method with an emphasis on planning and the division of labor offered an effective framework to organize the activities conducted within an organization (Morgan, 1997). In the work of sociologist Max Weber, a more comprehensive description of a bureaucracy emerged: an organization that is characterized by division of labor, managerial oversight, and the establishment of rules and regulations to govern behavior. Since then, from the body of research devoted to studying organizational development, three common elements have been cited to describe an organization: (1) people, (2) a goal or purpose, and (3) a structure (meaning any phenomenon created by the members of an organization) that defines and limits the behavior of members of an organization. Put simply, without people, a goal or purpose, and some form of structure, there is no organization! Of the three elements of an organization, *people* constitute the most important factor because without human beings the other two elements cease to exist. Once the three elements of an organization are brought together and an organization is formed, a culture develops. An organizational culture is the "way we do things around here" (Deal & Kennedy, 1982, p. 4).

The following are two more definitions of organizational culture:

> The pattern of basic assumptions that a given group has invented, discovered, or developed in learning to cope with its problems of external adaptation and internal integration. (Schein, 1983, p. 14)

> A set of symbols, ceremonies, and myths that communicates the underlying values and beliefs of that organization to its employees. (Ouchi, 1981, p. 41)

Moving beyond the definitional claims of organizational culture, we can use three workplace parameters to help us create a framework for measuring four distinct school cultures. A school's culture is important because the culture of a school influences every aspect of the learning process. The link between the culture of a school, the level of academic excellence, and the proposing of a course of action to improve the academic status of a school is contained in the SEMOC (see figure 12.2).

Three Workplace Parameters

The First Workplace Parameter: The Attitudes and Practices of Administrators

The attitudes and practices of administrators can be assessed by the overall degree of trust or lack of trust between administrative and nonadministrative personnel. An adversarial relationship between administrative and nonadministrative personnel tends to develop when administrators focus too much on operational and financial issues while ignoring or paying limited attention to the well-being of their employees. Dissatisfied employees purposely engage in many behaviors that reduce workplace performance and limit productivity. A fertile breeding ground for advancing workplace performance and productivity can only be laid when individuals are respected for who they are and placed in positions that complement their strengths. And make no mistake about it: Increasing productivity is the catalyst behind the socio-economic achievements of a society. William J. Baumol and Alan S. Blinder, in their book *Economics: Principles and Policy* (2000), put it this way:

> Only rising productivity can raise standards of living in the long run. Over long periods of time, small differences in rates of productivity growth compound like interest in a bank account and can make an enormous difference to a society's prosperity. Nothing contributes more to material well-being, to the reduction of poverty, to increases in leisure time, and to a country's ability to finance education, public health, environmental improvement, and the arts than its productivity growth rate. (p. 356)

From a strict organizational perspective, the right administrative attitude can breathe life into a management philosophy or culture that will boost the chances of academic success by establishing a school environment in which individuals will want to consistently perform at their best.

Administrative attitudes, practices, and policies that tend to have a negative impact specifically upon teacher performance are characterized by (a) inverse beginner responsibilities, (b) invisibility and isolation, (c) lack of professional dialogue, and (d) restricted choice (Glickman, 1985). Inverse beginner responsibilities occur when the newest teachers are given the most

School Culture A		
Measurement Criteria	**Academic Status of a School**	**Recommended Course of Action**
1. Trust 2. Cooperation 3. Task has meaning	Higher academic performance compared to other schools with similar resources.	Continue present policies and practices
School Culture B		
Two of the three "A" elements of school culture are present	Competitive academic performance compared to other schools with similar resources.	Incorporate the missing element of school culture "A" into the "B" culture
School Culture D		
One of the three "A" elements of school culture is present	Below-average academic performance compared to other schools with similar resources.	Incorporate the two missing elements of school culture "A" into the "D" culture
School Culture F		
1. Distrust 2. Non-cooperation 3. Task does not have meaning	Significantly below-average academic performance compared to other schools with similar resources.	Incorporate the three missing elements of school culture "A" into the "F" culture

Table 12.2: School Excellence Model of Organizational Culture

difficult tasks. Invisibility and isolation occur when teachers are not aware of how their teaching complements, reinforces, or negates the efforts of other teachers. Lack of professional dialogue refers to the shortage of time that teachers have to communicate with each other about academic and professional topics of interest as well as the lack of communication between administration and the teaching staff (Xin & MacMillan, 1999). Restricted choice reflects the situation that most teachers face: schedules that are set by administrators and curriculum selection determined by state and federal mandates. This restrictive work environment has been cited as a cause of teacher stress and poor health, which reduces the effectiveness of schools (Kelly & Colquhoun, 2003). Any administrative attitude, practice, or policy that negatively impacts teacher performance will tend to reduce the effectiveness of the learning environment.

The Second Workplace Parameter: The Organizational Environment among the Employees

The organizational environment among the employees in a workplace can be assessed by the extent of cooperation, internal politics, and favoritism within the organization. A highly politicized work environment will eat away at collegiality and undermine productivity. If left unchecked, it will eventually squelch innovation, cripple productivity, and destroy the organization. The long-term sustainability of any organization will depend on whether or not it controls internal politics and favoritism. Any organization that fails to base performance and compensation on merit will drift into mediocrity and possibly face extinction in a competitive environment. Merit must be rewarded; favoritism must be discouraged.

Establishing a learning community within your school can be an important step in creating a workplace where favoritism is discouraged while collegiality is encouraged. From Senge's (1990) definition of a learning organization, the claim can be made that a learning community exists when "collective aspirations are set free and where people are continually learning how to learn together" (cited in Zepeda, 1999, p. 59).

The Third Workplace Parameter: The Tasks Being Performed within an Organization

The tasks being performed within an organization can be assessed by asking whether a task has meaning for that individual. A recent study of 50,000 employees at 60 organizations found that most employees do not understand how their work contributes to the organization's goals and vision. On the other hand, organizations that create an environment where individuals feel that their work is important and that their organization is providing a positive benefit to the community set the stage for innovation and creativity. When innovation and creativity flourish, so does work performance and productivity. As teachers, administrators, and staff work together with a shared vision focused upon improving the learning environment, academic excellence can thrive. Increasing academic performance is the productivity yardstick by which to evaluate the quality of an educational environment. Enhanced academic excellence ultimately means a higher focus on understanding and promoting learning.

Measuring School Culture

Using the three workplace parameters as our base, we lay the foundation to identify four distinct school cultures:

School Culture A:

- There is a relationship of trust between administrative and nonadministrative personnel.
- Cooperation between individuals and departments/units is encouraged, and politicking and favoritism are discouraged. A learning community is established within the school.
- Individuals feel that their actions have a meaningful impact on the school and that their school stands for academic excellence and its policies are based upon ethical behavior and practices.

School Culture B:

- Two of the three elements of school culture A are present (e.g., trust and cooperation, however, the tasks might not have meaning for the individual).

School Culture D:

- One of the three elements of school culture A is present (e.g., the tasks might have meaning for the individual, but there is no trust or cooperation present within the culture of the school).

School Culture F:

- None of the three elements of school culture A are present.

Now that we have identified four measurable and distinct school cultures, we can present the SEMOC.

According to the SEMOC, schools that have a type-A culture are predicted to academically outperform other schools with similar resources. As for policy recommendations, the SEMOC suggests that administrative personnel should continue with their current practices.

Schools that have a type-B culture are predicted to be academically competitive with other schools with similar resources. The policy recommendation for these schools is to incorporate within their school culture the missing school-culture-A element and thus form a type-A culture.

Schools that have a type-D culture are predicted to be below-average academically performing schools. The policy recommendation for these schools is to develop a type-B or type-A school culture.

Schools that have a type-F culture are predicted to be significantly below-average academically performing schools. The policy recommendation for these schools is to incorporate the missing elements of organizational cultures B and A.

The SEMOC and the Bottom Line

The SEMOC links the culture of a school and the academic excellence of the school, ceteris paribus. In addition, the model provides school administrators with a methodology to improve the academic status of their school by adopting an administrative philosophy that fosters a type-A or type-B school culture. It elevates the analysis regarding school culture by quantifying the culture of a school in order to predict its academic performance while also providing a course of action to improve the school's culture and ultimately student learning.

The SEMOC and the "People Factor"

School cultures A, B, D, and F provide a framework for understanding academic performance—a framework built on three critical workplace parameters: the attitudes and practices of administrators, the organizational environment among the employees, and the tasks being performed within an organization. At the core of the SEMOC lies a common thread that binds each of the three critical workplace parameters together. This common thread is the driving force that ultimately determines whether or not a school will possess an A, B, D, or F culture and therefore its level of academic quality. So what is this common thread? The "people element" is the most important factor in any organization. The quality and attitudes of the people within a school set the stage for its accomplishments. A school district that invests in its employees will achieve a higher level of academic excellence and will produce a higher level of student learning. This investment in human capital must begin with the hiring process and continue throughout the employee's tenure with the school. A continual investment in human capital means providing a comprehensive and equitable employment package that, at the minimum, consists of a reasonable pay scale, benefits, and training.

To understand organizational performance, one must understand the "people factor" within an organization. The quality of an organization's people, at all levels, determines organizational success or failure because an organization is nothing more than the system(s) that the members of the organization create, and the superiority of any creation ultimately depends on the abilities of its creator(s). Thus, at the core of academic and school excellence is the quality of the members of the school. Failing to recognize this truism leaves the learning process and student achievement in peril.

THE CLASSROOM ENVIRONMENT

Presenting information in order to maximize learning begins with a desire on the part of the teacher to want to be in the classroom and actively engaged with the students in the learning process. The classroom environment should be about promoting learning—period.

Quality teaching is twofold: subject-matter expertise and pedagogy (the art of presenting subject-matter content). Too often teachers get so wrapped up in presenting the body of knowledge that pedagogy is a minor consideration. Teachers simply toss information to the students and basically leave it to them to sort through the complexity and try to make some sense of the material. Students with a low level of self-efficacy are lost in the process, left behind, and ultimately forgotten. In the end many students fail and leave the course with no more knowledge than when they started.

No student should ever be forgotten and left to fail. Students have different learning styles or preferences for dealing with intellectual tasks as well as different practical, creative, and analytical abilities. To increase the probability that learning will take place in the classroom, educators must utilize a variety of teaching methodologies. Various teaching methodologies include the following:

- The collaborative problem-solving (CPS) approach. The CPS approach has two components: problem-based learning and collaborative learning. Problem-based learning involves presenting students with a problem scenario. The students then work together in a collaborative effort to solve the problem.
- Service learning links academic coursework with community-service projects with the objective of improving each student's self-perception as well as fostering an appreciation of teamwork. As part of the service-learning project, students are expected to identify major issues relating to the subject they are studying, explore the fundamental theories connected with the subject, and provide evidence relating their experiences to the issues and theories that they have uncovered.
- Lecturing has its place in a teacher's repertoire, however, to maximize learning, the lecture method probably should not be exclusively utilized.
- Good lecturing in combination with student-centered learning activities or active student participation offers a positive learning alternative to the straightforward lecture method.
- Role-play simulations challenge students to process information efficiently, to rationally analyze various outcomes, to sharpen decision-making skills, and to improve their presentation skills.
- The inverted-classroom approach means that activities that have traditionally occurred inside the classroom can now take place outside the class-

room and vice versa. For example, lectures can be viewed outside of the classroom on a DVD while end-of-the-chapter questions usually assigned as homework can become the focal point within the classroom.

- Case studies examining a variety of situations pertinent to the subject matter being studied can be utilized in the classroom.
- Technology-based teaching methodologies, such as DVDs, CDs, various computer technologies, and the Internet, can be utilized to promote student academic success and understanding of the subject matter being explored.

Incorporating effective teaching methodologies in the classroom is a vital component of the learning process (Kohn, 2008). Being masters of pedagogy is critical if teachers are going to take an active role in promoting a quality learning environment. The following classroom principles can be utilized by teachers to craft a productive educational environment:

- Teachers must be committed to the idea that all students can learn something. "Your assumptions about learners will influence your expectations regarding what they can do" (Armstrong, Henson, & Savage, 2001, p. 109).
- Teachers need to be careful about grouping practices that place students into high-ability, intermediate-ability, and low-ability groups. Many times this type of grouping results in placing a disproportionate number of students from cultural and ethnic minorities into the low-ability groups. Each learning group "should constitute a representative racial, cultural, and gender sample of the entire class" (Armstrong, Henson, & Savage, 2001, p. 109).
- "Researchers have found that learners' cultural backgrounds influence their preference for a given instructional style" (Grant & Sleeter, 1994, cited in Armstrong, Henson, & Savage, 2001, p. 109). Lessons must be planned that allow students to approach and understand the subject matter in different ways by utilizing a variety of teaching methodologies.
- Teachers must be aware of their own world views and experiences and how their world view impacts what they think the world is all about and what constitutes proper learning approaches.
- Teachers must avoid favoritism in the classroom. They should strive for equity in their relationships with students and provide encouragement to all; a teacher's credibility depends upon these factors (Armstrong, Henson, & Savage, 2001).

Education is all about understanding and promoting learning. A focus upon the characteristics of each student means a focus upon how information is presented to students, the pedagogies utilized in the classroom. Teachers that focus upon the needs of their students and adjust their teaching methodologies accordingly have begun the process of enhancing the learning environment. In the final analysis, isn't promoting learning the ultimate objective of all teachers?

THE FACILITIES WHERE LEARNING IS TO TAKE PLACE

Learning opportunities can be interwoven into the physical structure of a school, making the building and grounds an integral part of the learning process. According to Bunting, Li, Locke, and Nair (2005), throughout time educational systems have been aligned for four purposes: (1) socialization, (2) vocation, (3) self-fulfillment, and (4) transformation. Socialization involves replicating society to imbue local and national culture as well as to promote citizenship. Vocation focuses upon training people for employment. Self-fulfillment deals with developing individuals to their maximum potential. Transformation relates to providing equal opportunity for learning and fostering change for a better world.

The following principles serve as a guide for merging building design with maximizing the learning environment (Bunting, Li, Locke, & Nair, 2005):

- Does the building layout elicit a feeling of belonging and community?
- Are the developmental abilities among children respected by separating the younger from the older students?
- Have long corridors been replaced by "learning streets" and other areas that promote socialization and provide opportunities for informal learning?
- Are the common and community spaces designed to be used before, during, and after school hours without disrupting the academic areas?
- Do all classrooms and other learning areas have adequate natural light, and are the classroom wings oriented toward east-west direction?
- Has the media center been designed to support reading and small-group work?
- Are there comfortable areas within and around the school that encourage independent study and reading for pleasure?
- Do the students have access to food and beverages in formal and informal zones (cafes instead of cafeterias)?
- Is there access to appropriate educational technologies within and outside the classroom?
- Are there opportunities to create outdoor learning experiences?
- Does the building design provide opportunities for team teaching, peer tutoring, and interdisciplinary curricula projects?

- Does the design allow for reconfiguration of spaces on a daily basis and allow for more significant changes over time?
- Does the building serve as a community center?
- Are the laboratories and other specialty rooms designed with flexibility?
- Is there a home base for every student? In the higher grades, this might be a workstation, and in lower or middle grades, it might be a locker.

COMPLETING THE PICTURE: AN EFFECTIVE LEARNING ENVIRONMENT

An effective learning environment is created when the characteristics of an effective educational leader are combined with the elements of the SEMOC, productive classroom techniques, and the principles of effective building design.

CRITICAL POINTS TO REMEMBER

- The structural environment of education refers to the variables under the control or influence of a school. Key structural characteristics that impact learning include (a) the leadership at a school, (b) the school's culture, (c) the classroom environment, and (d) the facilities in which the learning process takes place.
- Effective educational leaders create an environment where learning takes center stage.
- The School Excellence Model of Organizational Culture (SEMOC) identifies four specific school cultures and provides a framework for predicting academic performance based upon the school culture.
- Quality teaching is about knowing course content and promoting learning.
- Learning opportunities can be interwoven into the physical structure of a school, making building and landscape design an integral part of the learning process.

REFERENCES

Armstrong, D., Henson, K., & Savage, T. (2001). *Teaching today: A introduction for education.* 6th ed. Upper Saddle River, NJ: Merrill/Prentice Hall.

Baumol, W. J., and Blinder, A. S. (2000). *Economics: Principles and Policy.* Orlando, FL: Harcourt College Publishers.

Bunting, A., Li, P., Locke, J., & Nair, P. (2005). Creating 21st century learning environments. [Electronic version]. *PEB Exchange*, 55, pp. 15–26.

Crosby, P. (1989). *Running things: The art of making things happen.* New York: Mentor.

Deal, T. E., & Kennedy, A. A. (1982). *Corporate cultures: The rites and rituals of corporate life.* Reading, MA: Addison-Wesley.

Glickman, C. (1985). The supervisor's challenge: Changing the teacher's work environment. *Educational Leadership*, 42, pp. 38–41.

Grant, C., & Sleeter, C. (1994). *Making choices for multicultural education: Five approaches to race, class, and gender.* New York: Maxwell Macmillan International.

Johnson, Jr., J. (2005). Preparing educational leaders to close achievement gaps. *Theory into Practice*, 44(1), pp. 45–52. Retrieved February 24, 2006, from EBSCO host research database.

Kelly, P., & Colquhoun, D. (2003). Governing the stressed self: Teacher health and well-being and effective schools. *Discourse Studies in the Cultural Politics of Education*, 24, pp. 191–204.

Kohn, A. (2008). It's not what we teach. *Education Week*, 28(3), pp. 26, 32.

Morgan, G. (1997). *Images of organization.* 2nd ed. Thousand Oaks, CA: Sage.

Ouchi, W. G. (1981). *Theory Z: How American business can meet the Japanese challenge.* Reading, MA: Addison-Wesley.

Schein, E. H. (1983, Summer). The role of the founder in creating organizational culture. *Organizational Dynamics*, pp. 13–28.

Senge, P. (1990). *The fifth discipline: The art and practice of the learning organization.* New York: Currency Doubleday.

Xin, M., & MacMillan, R. B. (1999). Influences of workplace conditions on teachers' job satisfaction. *Journal of Educational Research*, 93, pp. 39–48.

Zepeda, S. (1999). *Staff development: Practices that promote leadership in learning communities.* Larchmont, NY: Eye on Education.

Chapter Thirteen

Societal and Community Characteristics

To learn where you're going, you have to know where you've come from.
—James Cobb (2007, p. 315)

Heredity refers to factors that are determined at conception and include physical stature, facial attractiveness, gender, temperament, energy level, and other biological and physiological factors. An individual's social environment includes the culture in which an individual is raised, family norms, friends, social groups, and other influences that we experience in life. For every individual, our heredity and social environment influence in some way our capacity to absorb knowledge, develop skills, and improve our abilities. As denoted by Back and Monroe (1985) and Jansen (1995), a seminal study conducted by Coleman and colleagues (1966) concluded that the socio-economic factors of a student have more impact upon student performance than any other factor.

In 1998, Toutkoushian and Taylor concluded that socio-economic factors (which are beyond the control of the school) are a major factor impacting student performance. In their study, they utilized data on student achievement at public high schools in New Hampshire. Multiple regression or truncated regression analysis was utilized depending upon the variable to be explained. From the literature, the authors noted that various socioeconomic factors, including the percentage of students from low-income families, are highly correlated with poor school outcomes. However, it is not universally accepted that schools located in low socioeconomic areas cannot perform at a high level. Toutkoushian and Taylor focused upon three socioeconomic factors: (a) unemployment rate for a school district, (b) percentage of adults in the district with at least a bachelor's degree, and (c) percentage of district students who were eligible for free or reduced-price meals. These socioeconomic factors were found to account for approximately half of the variation among schools regarding standardized tests scores and the propensity of a student to consider a college education.

Of all the socioeconomic factors that impact student achievement, the lack of parental support has been cited as a primary factor impacting educational outcomes. "Nearly 90% of the variance on student math tests can be predicted without knowing anything about the school; one only needs to know the number of parents in the home, the education level of the parents, the community in which the family lives, and the state's poverty rate" (Robinson and Brandon, 1994, cited by Evans, 2005, p. 584). "Schooling is a relatively 'weak treatment,' responsible, in most cases, for no more than 25% of the total outcome, if that" (Gallagher, 1998, cited by Evans, 2005, p. 584).

Whether students learn depends not only on "what happens in school, but on the experiences, habits, values, and ideas they acquire from the environment in which they live" (Csikszentmihalyi, 1995, cited by Evans, 2005). There can be no question that societal and community characteristics impact the learning process.

CRITICAL POINT TO REMEMBER

- Societal and community characteristics must be factored into the equation when determining the effectiveness of a learning environment.

REFERENCES

Back, J., & Monroe, E. (1985). The effective schools concept: An effective way to help schools make a difference? [Electronic version]. *Education*, 105(3), pp. 232–236.

Cobb, J. (2007). *The arctic event*. New York: Vision/Hachette Book Group.

Coleman, J., Campbell, E., Hobson, C., McPartland, J., Mood, A., Weinfeld, F., & York, R. (1966). *Equality of educational opportunity*. Washington, DC: U.S. Government Printing Office.

Csikszentmihalyi, M. (1995, Fall). Education for the twenty-first century. *Daedalus*, p. 107.

Evans, R. (2005). Reframing the achievement gap. [Electronic version]. *Phi Delta Kappan*, 86(8), pp. 582–589.

Gallagher, James. (1998). Education alone is a weak treatment. *Education Weekly*, 8 July, pp. 43, 60.

Jansen, J. (1995). Effective schools? *Comparative Education*, 31(2), pp. 181–200. Retrieved October 7, 2005, from EBSCO host research databases.

Robinson, Glen E., and Brandon, David P. (1994). *NAEP test scores: Should they be used to compare and rank state educational quality?* Arlington, Va.: Educational Research Service.

Toutkoushian, R. K., & Taylor, C. (1998). Effects of socioeconomic factors on public high school outcomes and rankings. [Electronic version]. *The Journal of Educational Research*, 98(5), pp. 259–271.

Chapter Fourteen

What about Maximizing Student Learning?

To explain, Amy would have to open door after door into herself, into places in the heart that she did not want to visit.

—Dean Koontz (2007, p. 44)

Students unwilling to put forth the time and effort that is required to learn dramatically reduce the probability that they will learn. The learning goals that a student chooses are influenced by the background of the student, especially the student's perception of his capability to handle a particular learning task. A student's self-efficacy affects his motivation, choice of goals, expectations of success, and attributions for success or failure. A student with high levels of self-efficacy tends to select task mastery goals or doing what is necessary to learn the information and develop the skills that are required to accomplish the learning task. Performance-approach goals tend to also be selected by students with high levels of self-efficacy because these students are interested in demonstrating to their teachers and peers their intellectual capability to outperform most other students.

On the other hand, students with low levels of self-efficacy tend to select performance-avoidance goals, which involve reducing the possibility of failure by avoiding novel and challenging tasks or cheating. In addition, students with low levels of self-efficacy may engage in self-handicapping behaviors in order to blame performance outcomes on the circumstances rather than on their ability. What can be summarized regarding self-efficacy is that students with high levels of self-efficacy expect positive educational outcomes and attribute the outcome to their own ability and effort; the opposite is true for students with low levels of self-efficacy. Ultimately it is every student's decision to want to learn or not. It is a personal decision, and to ignore this fact is a denial of reality. As previously stated, denying reality never leads to anything positive.

Besides a student's willingness to learn, another educational reality that impacts the learning environment is the frequency with which a student changes schools for reasons other than normal progression from one level of schooling to the next (Jacobson, 2001). As reported by Jacobson, a 1993 study found that students who changed schools at least six times between first and twelfth grade were 35% more likely to fail, while another study from 1995 found that by the sixth grade the students who frequently moved from school to school tended to be a full year behind other students. Additionally, it was reported by Jacobson that students who change schools need between 6 to 18 months to regain a sense of equilibrium, security, and control. A student's mobility and decision to want to learn or not learn are powerful variables that influence the learning process.

CRITICAL POINT TO REMEMBER

• The bottom line is that the student is responsible for his or her own learning. Those who make the decision to want to learn and then put forth the time and effort necessary to learn will increase the probability that they will ultimately succeed.

REFERENCES

Jacobson, L. (2001). Moving targets. *Education Week*, 20(29), pp. 32–35. Retrieved February 15, 2006, from EBSCO host research database.
Koontz, D. (2007). *The darkest evening of the year*. New York: Bantam.

Chapter Fifteen

The Final Message

Life is like a great carpet. Seen from one side of a loom, it makes no sense. It has no shape, no logic. Just hundreds of strands of wool hanging loosely here and there. But seen from the other side, everything can be understood. The pattern becomes clear. There are no loose bits of wool. Just order.

—Philip Kerr (1997, p. 357)

The pattern of the road before him was chaos. He could not know where it would lead.

—Dean Koontz (2007b, p. 19)

At the core of every ordered system, whether a family or factory, is chaos. But in the whirl of every chaos lies a strange order, waiting to be found.

—Dean Koontz (2007a, p. 18)

To come to grips with a chaotic system and attempt to bring order, one must deal with the reality of the situation; anything else is foolishness. So let's be clear and deal with reality. To improve the educational system, we must understand the following truisms:

- The "business or mission of education" is about understanding and promoting learning, no other social agenda or political ideology. Learning is strictly defined as acquiring new knowledge, skills, and/or abilities.
- Any proposal for improving the educational process must flow from the realities associated with education and learning.
- The structural environment of education as outlined in this book should be focused on maximizing the learning process, not maximizing student learning. The structural environment of education cannot maximize student learning. Maximizing student learning might be a byproduct of maximizing the learning process.

- The student is ultimately responsible for his or her learning by making the decision to want to learn; only a student who wants to learn, despite everything else, will be on the path to maximizing his or her learning.

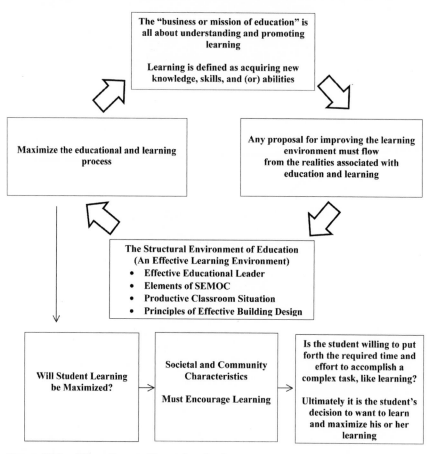

Figure 15.1.   Education and Learning Cycle

As illustrated by the education and learning cycle, in the final analysis, the widely accepted view of most educators, politicians, and the public that the educational system exists to maximize student learning is a myth. The educational system at its best can only provide an effective and efficient overall learning environment. Beyond that, the ultimate determinants of whether student learning will be maximized are embedded within the character of the student and the environment in which the student lives. Failing to accept this reality has led to an underperforming education system and ineffective educational policies. The choice is to continue to wander down a path leading to nowhere or to jump onto a new path that changes the direction of education policy, a change of direction that deals with reality and moves us toward an educational system that works.

CRITICAL POINTS TO REMEMBER FROM THE BOOK

- Educators and political decision makers must understand that the purpose or mission of education and the roles of students and teachers have gotten lost among the cluster of educational ideologies and political crosscurrents that have evolved. In other words, education has lost its identity. To restore its identity, the field of education must return to its roots, meaning that any procedure, theory, or practice should be focused upon the purpose or mission of education as outlined in this book. Political ideologies and social agendas must be put aside so the true mission of education can be achieved. Political ideologies and social agendas do not constitute a body of knowledge for learning. Only from the body of knowledge within an academic field can learning spring forth, like the petals of a flower gracefully opening on a bright, sunny day.
- Educators and political decision makers must acknowledge the fact that learning is acquiring new knowledge, skills, and/or abilities. Education does not exist to take care of other societal problems or issues. The expansion of a body of knowledge in an academic field or increasing the skill and/or ability levels of individuals within an academic field lies at the heart of the educational process.
- Educators and political decision makers must acknowledge that learning is a complex task. Students must put forth effort, be persistent, and spend enormous amounts of time if they are going to learn. Even then, no one is guaranteed that he will be successful and improve his knowledge, skills, and/or abilities. What is for certain is that if a student decides not to learn, learning will not occur.
- A highly qualified teacher is a lifelong learner who knows subject content and can inspire students to learn. A teacher who loves to learn can ignite that same passion for learning in her students. If one does not love to learn and increase her knowledge, skills, and/or abilities, then why would that person want to be in education?
- Educators and political decision makers must acknowledge that a student's decision about how much time and effort he or she is willing to put forth is a critical factor impacting learning. A student who feels that education and learning are not important will dramatically reduce what will be learned. The ultimate decision to learn rests with the student. A student who truly wants to learn will overcome any obstacle. That's why some students can succeed in an ineffective educational environment while other students might fail in the best educational situation. By the way, a

student's decision to want to learn or not learn does not excuse educators from trying to build a positive structural environment for learning. Certainly the chances of achieving academic success are higher in an effective and efficient educational environment. However, the bottom line is quite clear: Only those students willing to do what is necessary to academically succeed will have an opportunity to succeed.

- Educators and political decision makers must come to grips with the fact that whether a student will learn is influenced by the social and family environment in which the student lives.
- An effective learning environment consists of: (1) an effective educational leader, (2) the elements of the School Excellence Model of Organizational Culture (SEMOC), (3) a productive classroom situation, and (4) the principles of effective building design.
- Educators and political decision makers must make sure that per-pupil expenditure is fairly distributed to ensure that all students have an equal opportunity to learn. This means dividing all property taxes collected for education and then dividing that monetary total by the total number of students so that every school district gets the same amount of financial support per-pupil. The debate should not be about traditional schools versus charter schools and financially robbing from Peter to pay Paul. The issue is about equal per-pupil funding.
- The leaks along the P–16 educational pipeline must be fixed. The correction process must start with P–12 because everything begins there. In a system, if any segment of the system is not properly functioning, the rest of the system is doomed to fail. This is a basic premise of systems theory. The reason that so many students entering higher education have to take developmental courses is obvious; the elementary and secondary education segment of the educational pipeline is not functioning properly.
- Understanding the education and learning cycle can lead to improving the educational environment, for the realties and truisms of the educational process are illustrated within the cycle. To improve any system, one must deal with the realities of that system. For those who continue to ignore the realities of education and learning, why are they surprised that the educational system is underperforming?
- Never forget Milton Friedman's (n.d.) policy statement, "One of the great mistakes is to judge policies and programs by their intentions rather than their results." When we forget this ultimate truism, any public policy, including education, will never be headed in the proper direction. So let's change course and accept reality for what it is and base education policy upon reality.

REFERENCES

Friedman, M. (n.d.). Retrieved September 18, 2012, from http://sphotos-a.xx.fbcdn.net/hphotos-prn1/550493_10100414629650916_473350904_n.jpg.

Kerr, P. (1997). *Esau: A thriller*. New York: Henry Holt.

Koontz, D. (2007a). *The darkest evening of the year*. New York: Bantam.

Koontz, D. (2007b). *The good guy*. New York: Bantam.